URBAN PLAYGROUNDS

*ATHLETES CLAIM CITIES
AROUND THE WORLD*

gestalten

PLAYTIME

WELCOME TO THE WORLD OF URBAN SPORTS

Over the last 70 years, a small handful of sports have revolutionized how humans interact with the urban environment. Born from the innovative minds of teenagers and young adults frustrated by inconsistent Pacific waves, or not being old enough to ride off-road motorbikes in the hills of California, skateboarding and BMX have evolved from niche activities undertaken in small pockets of the United States into respected, mainstream sports now included in the Olympics.

Following in the desire lines created by these pioneering alternative sports, other pursuits have followed, including parkour, rollerblading, and freerunning, transforming cities into fully-fledged playgrounds in the process. From the centuries-old marble slabs found in the plazas and squares of European cities to the 20th-century cement structures dreamt up by master architects and municipal offices alike, planners, architects, and designers have unknowingly (and more recently knowingly) constructed the perfect environment for urban sports. When riders and skaters demonstrated an alternative use for the building blocks of city life—a set of stairs ripe for gapping, a handrail perfect for grinding—the establishment viewed it at first as an unwelcome disruption to the accepted uses of urban space. Local governments responded with dismay, treating these new expressions of creativity as acts of criminal damage, sometimes banning them in public spaces or enforcing curfews and legislation against them. True to their founding spirit though, skaters and BMXers took this as just another hurdle to overcome in their pursuit of new and unridden spots.

In some cities, compromises such as designated skateparks were provided to give these flourishing sports a home—far enough away to ensure they couldn't bother the rest of society. But over time, poorly maintained facilities and waning popularity moved the dedicated core of the sports' subcultures back once more to street spots, albeit ones so disused and dilapidated that the presence of skaters and BMXers was unlikely to ruffle any feathers.

This committed minority helped lay the groundwork for the urban sports we know and love today. In the 1980s and '90s, an ever-growing number of youth-focused cultural vehicles—MTV, underground magazines, video games—made urban sports aspirational to young and impressionable kids outside of their original audience. As athletes like Tony Hawk and Mat Hoffman consistently raised the bar in their respective fields, generations of future skaters and BMXers were inspired to drop into a quarterpipe or hit a ramp for the first time. The result was an explosion in popularity that has propelled these sports into the mainstream ever since.

The phenomenon hasn't remained limited to younger audiences with no political clout. As kids who were exposed to the early iterations of skateboarding and BMX became adults and (in some cases) influential decision-makers, the friction between the authorities and alternative subcultures has softened. The outside impression of these subcultures has gradually shifted from delinquents who were up to no good to acrobats on wheels. In areas where riding would previously have been banned, spaces have started to open up. Meanwhile, DIY street spots that have long been at the heart of communities, such as the Undercroft at London's Southbank Centre or Portland's Burnside skatepark, now have official protection from the wrecking ball.

From the roots of each discipline and their appropriation of public spaces to the ways that architects, planners, and public and private enterprises have responded to them, this book charts the rise of urban sports around the globe and the individuals and groups who have made them the global phenomena they are today. These many subcultures are in no way homogenous, and each has found a way to flourish within set parameters. From the cities on the U.S. West Coast where the sports were conceived to the burgeoning scenes of Dubai or Lagos, each has its own story to tell, with unique urban fabrics, architecture, and athletes who have cut their teeth (literally, in some cases) on the iconic features of these equally iconic places.

Ultimately, *Urban Playgrounds* is a snapshot of a world where alternative expressions of creativity are now mentioned in the same breath as mainstream sports— and which are now fully inscribed into the urban topography.

—**Charlie Allenby**

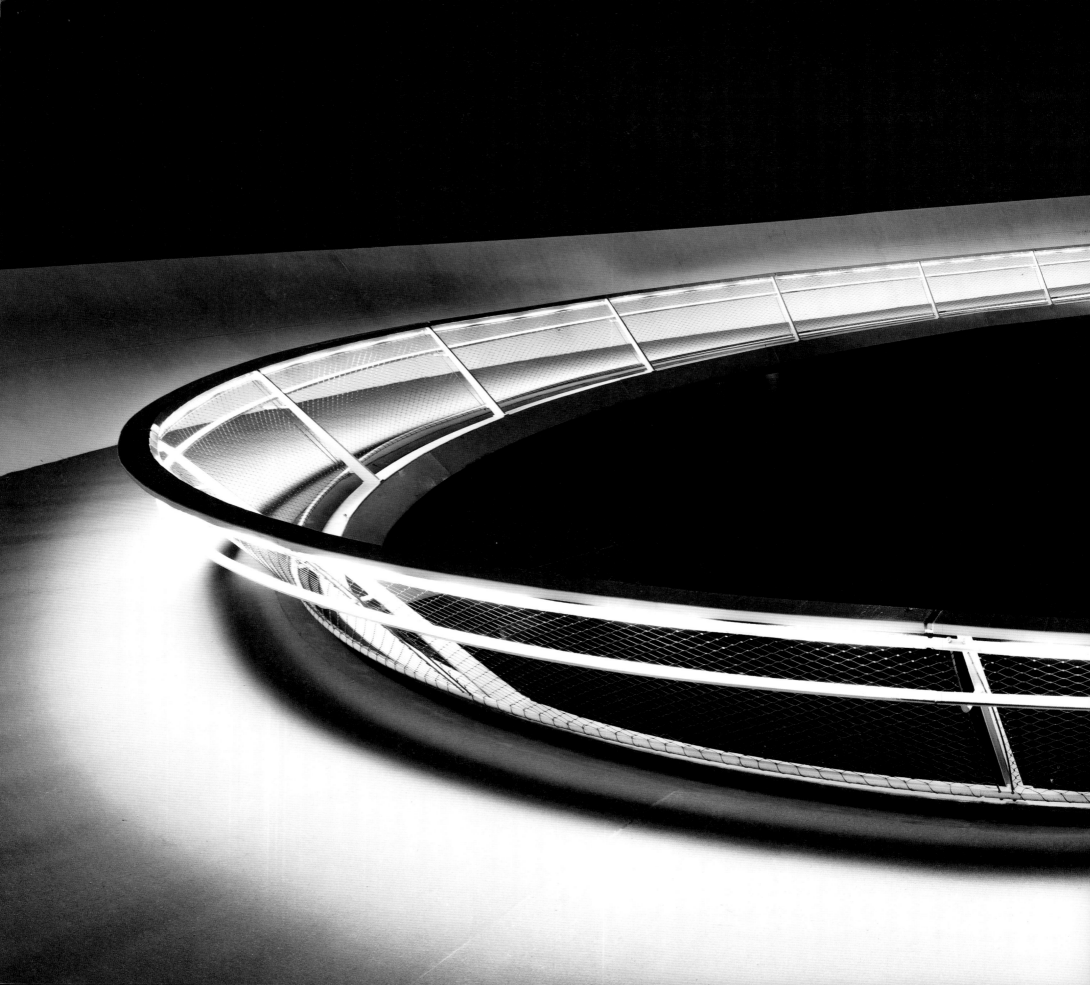

OUT ON THE TILES

*EXPLORING THE SCENIC BACKDROPS AND
NIGHT-RIDING OPTIONS OF BALMY LISBON*

Like their Iberian cousins, the locals of Lisbon take a relaxed approach to skate and BMX. It's not uncommon to stumble across a plaza with a feature worth hitting, but the most popular locations include the Tejo Promenade in the shadows of Ponte 25 de Abril, or the ledges and rails of the university. For vert action, there's a famous street quarterpipe on Rua de São Tomé in the old town of Alfama that's adorned with artist Vhils's mosaic-style tribute to fado singer Amália Rodrigues. Pictured here is French-born flatland artist Matthias Dandois performing tricks against the city's famed cobblestones.

Lisbon also has a host of modern and well-maintained skateparks. Monsanto, Bairro Horizonte, and Campolide attract athletes in the center, while Parque das Gerações is an ideal outdoor skatepark for day trips west along the coast toward Cascais.

Come summer, the city suffers from two things—heat and tourists. Most skaters and BMXers stick to riding into the long, warm nights, avoiding boiling temperatures and legions of pedestrians at the same time. It's also a city built on seven hills, which is where the hop-on, hop-off trams come into their own as they ferry athletes to each spot, allowing them to save their energy for the real run.

FREERUNNING IN VENICE

PASHA PETKUNS USES HIS PARKOUR SKILLS IN A
ROMANTIC RACE THROUGH THE CITY'S CANALS

With its narrow, crowded streets and crisscrossing canals, Venice doesn't immediately come to mind as a free-running destination. But as Latvian freerunner Pasha Petkuns shows in his 2018 Red Bull film *Chasing Love in Venice,* the city is packed with buildings, obstacles, and backdrops that make it a unique location for practicing parkour. In the film, Petkuns launches himself onto moving gondolas, twists and spins across bridges, and even leaps from a gondola over a footbridge and back onto the same boat.

"Venice is one of the most magical and beautiful cities," he says. "I've traveled to many places, but Venice is one of the few to really embrace the freedom of movement that's in free-running and parkour. Being given the chance to do parkour there made it an adventure I'll never forget."

The city famed for romance contains numerous scenic freerunning spots, including more than 400 bridges to climb and play on. Freerunners can also tumble and backflip through the pigeons in St. Mark's Square, beneath the bell tower of St. Mark's Campanile, or follow Petkuns and vault walls and sprint along the jetty in front of the Church of Sant'Alvise. Tumbling along the paving stones in front of the Punta della Dogana art museum, with the Grand and Giudecca Canals shimmering a few feet away, is an experience unlike any other. "I felt like a superhero, being able to fly around one of the world's most iconic cities," Petkuns says. "I felt like I could embody the city and truly be one with it."

AN ODE TO BERLIN

*EXPLORING THE NATURAL TRANSITIONS AND
MARBLE PLAYGROUNDS OF THE GERMAN CAPITAL*

Internationally known as a techno paradise, Berlin has much more to offer than clubs that never close. The capital of Germany and one of the street-art capitals of the world, Berlin thrives off a rich culture forged from a turbulent past. Berlin's regeneration since the Second World War and the fall of the Berlin Wall in 1989 has led to an incredible juxtaposition of new and old architecture. Cobblestones line the streets, yet marble covers the plazas. A city steeped in history from the past 100 years alone, Berlin also boasts a somewhat relaxed environment with a relatively nonchalant approach to doing whatever one pleases.

Spots are in abundance, with every district, or *Kiez,* offering a unique selection of both crust and perfection. Berlin is home to many large monuments, usually found within the city's numerous green spaces and parks: the Memorial to Polish Soldiers and German Anti-Fascists, housed within Volkspark Friedrichshain, is a famous spot, well known in the skateboarding world for its three consecutive stair sets and ledges.

Berlin's jewel in the crown is Kulturforum—a collection of cultural buildings housing some of the best-known spots for a mix of extreme sports. Built between the 1950s and 1990s in the west of the city and designed by architects including Hans Scharoun and Ludwig Mies van der Rohe, with its marble plaza consisting of perfect ledges, banks, and an infamous double set, the Kulturforum is a sure stop on any rider's checklist.

Tempelhofer Feld, the former airport which lies just 20 minutes from the center of Berlin, is now a public park for activities of all types, including kite-boarding, roller-skating, skateboarding, and BMX. The skatepark built on the Feld was created using stones from the former GDR Palace of the Republic, and recreates several iconic street spots that are no longer accessible in Berlin.

Boasting a thriving DIY scene alongside marble playgrounds, Berlin's relatively new creation, the Greifswalder DIY, has become a popular spot for extreme sports. Tight transitions and daily BBQ sessions have cemented a unique identity that tips its cap to the American DIY greats, while remaining true to its Berlin roots.

Rough sidewalks and cracked pavement make skating from spot to spot pretty unforgiving, so the best way to reach them is by bike. The weather in Berlin varies from Baltic winters, with canals and lakes occasionally freezing over, to scorching summers—fortunately, in the colder months, the indoor concrete *Skatehalle* (skatepark) in Friedrichshain has you covered.

HELL RIDE

STRANGER THINGS AT TEUFELSBERG

A dark forest, pale moonlight, wisps of fog …
This is the spooky backdrop for a virtuoso
performance by Bruno Hoffmann, one of
Germany's best street BMX bikers, in the legendary *Devil's Voice* video from 2017.
          The setting is an eerily beautiful location
in the western part of Berlin: the Teufelsberg.
Mysterious ruins crown the 400-ft. (120-m)
hill: abandoned towers with strange domes,
dilapidated buildings, all completely covered
with graffiti. Decades of decay have made
the area a popular playground for the international street-art scene, and for mountain
bikers who enjoy letting off steam on the (not
entirely legal) trails.
          The tumultuous history of the Teufels-
berg adds the finishing touch to the spectacle.
In the 1940s, the unfinished skeleton of a Nazi
military college once stood on this site. Later,
the rubble from a third of Berlin's destroyed
buildings was dumped here. During the Cold
War, the Americans set up a listening station
on the mountain of rubble, whose domes were
designed by the futurist R. Buckminster Fuller.
The facilities have stood empty since 1999;
for street biker Hoffmann, it was the perfect
environment for his hell ride.

RUNNING REVERSE

BACK TO THE ROOTS OF FRANKFURT'S UNIQUE FREERUNNING SCENE

On the one hand, Frankfurt is a financial metropolis, famous in Germany for its skyline; on the other it is home to one of the most active urban sports scenes in the country. Skaters, BMX riders, parkour athletes, and freerunners form a close-knit, vibrant community. Frankfurt-born Jason Paul, considered one of the most famous freerunners in the world, travels around the globe in pursuit of crazy new stunts. But in 2019, he returned home to the city where it all began, literally turning back the clock for his video *Running Reverse,* which saw him perform his freerunning routine backwards. With a seemingly endless motivation to anchor the sport in his hometown

and share his passion, Paul is one of the founding fathers of Frankfurt's exciting freerunning scene.

Although the city may not have the coolest spots, the community itself makes the local scene unique—and word has spread globally. Now, when international freerunners come to Germany, a stop in Frankfurt is a must. It's one of the reasons Paul keeps coming back to where his international career began. He was 14 years old when a TV documentary introduced him to parkour, and though he had never heard of it before, he knew instantly that this synthesis of sports and art, explosiveness and style, was exactly where he felt right at home.

JASON PAUL

Jason, you are a Frankfurt native. You grew up in the city and laid the foundation for your international career here. What is special about Frankfurt am Main?

Jason Paul: We simply have the most vibrant parkour community that I could ever imagine. Our sport actually thrives on obstacles, challenging spots, and in this regard other cities such as Berlin, Munich, and Lisbon—cities with ideal spots that I'm familiar with—are way ahead of us. But the scene itself makes a huge difference. In Frankfurt, we have a large and very active community that does a lot together. Although there are certainly more freerunners in Berlin and Munich, they tend to be organized in small groups, whereas in Frankfurt it's a big cohesive whole, regardless of your age or how good you are. The WhatsApp group is full to bursting, and people just send out a message spontaneously to see if anyone else feels like training.

You started parkour when you were 14, at a time when only the extreme insiders knew what it was all about. How did it work back then?

Jason Paul: I saw on TV how these people were jumping over railings, scaffolding, benches, and construction fences in Parisian suburbs and were crossing the city like that. That deeply fascinated me from the very first second. I started learning parkour techniques, and I teamed up with others who were just as crazy about it as I was so we could train together.

So you all literally built the Frankfurt parkour scene from nothing?

Jason Paul: It all kind of went hand in hand. Some people found each other, we held the first meetings, and we got to know our city again from a completely new perspective. That's how it all started. The community kept growing, and we got better and better … We kicked off a perpetual-motion machine back then.

Which spots should definitely not be missed in Frankfurt?

Jason Paul: The Finanzamt, Hauptwache, and Ostpark: these are the absolute classics in Frankfurt am Main.

THE INITIAL SPARK

THE BIRTHPLACE OF THE URBAN SPORTS SCENE IN THE NETHERLANDS

In the 1970s, the urban sports movement took off in the Netherlands, with 1977 considered to mark the beginning of the Dutch skating scene. Waterlooplein, a square in the Groot Waterloo district of Amsterdam, became the melting pot of the fledgling skate movement and played a pivotal role in the local scene's development. Skateboarders built the country's first halfpipe in the square, which at the time was undergoing massive changes due to the construction of the subway. Anyone in the Netherlands who skated or wanted to do tricks on roller skates made a pilgrimage to Waterlooplein— until it was redeveloped for the construction of the Stopera building complex, encompassing the city hall and opera house.

As its popularity grew, urban sports became an entrenched part of youth culture. This still holds true, and today every major Dutch city features dedicated spaces for skaters, BMX riders, and parkour athletes. There are scarcely any districts in Amsterdam, Rotterdam, or Eindhoven that do not have designated places where athletes can meet and work on their skills. Area 51 in Eindhoven, for example, is the largest indoor skatepark in the Benelux countries and has become a vital meeting place for athletes, as well as a cultural hot spot featuring sports, dance, art, and music under one roof.

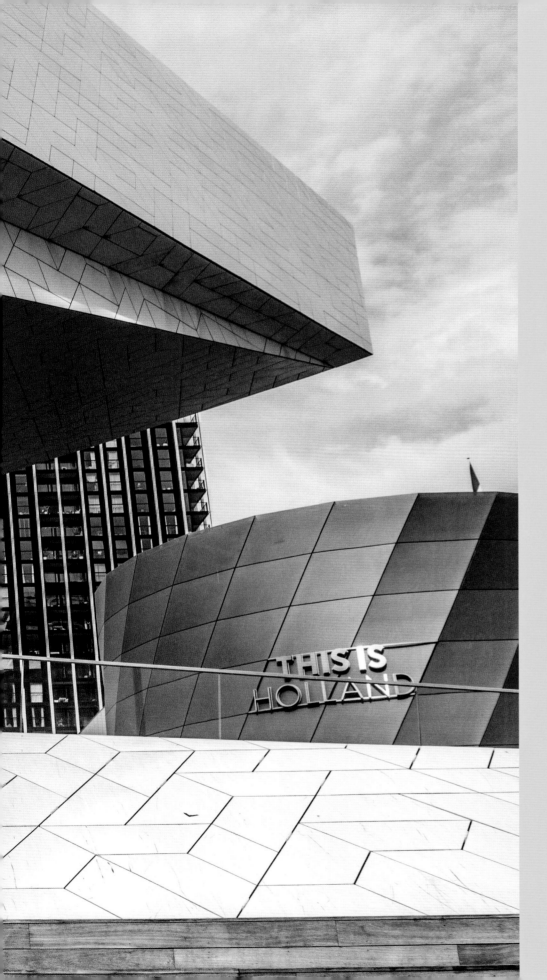

RED BULL 100 HOURS

SIX ATHLETES, THREE FILMMAKERS, ONE VIDEO:
FREERUNNING STARS TAKE ON A UNIQUE CHALLENGE

Red Bull 100 Hours in Amsterdam was a unique freerunning event that demanded the utmost from the very best parkour athletes in the world. The brief was as simple as it was challenging: three teams, each consisting of two freerunners and one filmmaker, were given 100 hours to develop, plan, and film their ideas during the 2018 Koningsdag national holiday. There was no time for lengthy location scouting or extensive planning, simply a fast shoot that pushed both freerunners and filmmakers to their (creative) limits. The event took the teams straight through the city, from the revelers on the canals and squares of the old city center to new architectural icons, such as the Eye Filmmuseum by Delugan Meissl Associated Architects. Looking for jumps and guided by their intuition and instinct for improvisation, Red Bull 100 Hours had something original and pure that was very close to the basic philosophy of the scene, deservedly attracting widespread international acclaim.

CITY OF HIGHLIGHTS

*SKATERS AND RIDERS COLLIDE WITH HISTORY
ON THE STREETS OF PARIS*

Despite its relatively small size, Paris has a strong urban sports scene and a diverse array of street and park spots to choose from, regardless of ability or discipline. The city's centuries-old squares, legendary landmarks, and cobblestone streets provide a thrilling backdrop to any session.

With its curbs, benches, and Volcom funbox, Paris's best-known spot is the Place de la République. Although the square dates back to 1811, its current form took shape after a major redevelopment project at the start of the 2010s. When it reopened in 2013, the square had been transformed from a "glorified roundabout," as the then-mayor described it, into a huge, pedestrianized space that garnered finalist status in the 2014 edition of the European Prize for Urban Public Space. Located on the border between the 3rd, 10th, and 11th arrondissements, with excellent public transport connections, it also has an ingrained alternative vibe, thanks to being a de facto meeting point for Parisian protests.

The Place de la République is just the tip of the iceberg when it comes to amazing Parisian squares. Whether channeling Matthias Dandois by practicing flatland beneath the Place de la Bastille's July Column, or hitting the stair sets at the Palais de Tokyo—the stunning two-winged art deco building that is a home of contemporary art in Paris—the backdrops are second to none. Between sessions, riders flock to the Place des Vosges—the city's oldest planned square—to soak up the atmosphere beneath the ornate porticos.

When it comes to parks, the French capital has plentiful options. Its most iconic is also probably its smallest; the concrete bowl and cradle by Austrian artist Peter Kogler in Square Robert-Bajac, next to Porte d'Italie, offer a unique challenge riders of all levels, and that's before considering its hypnotic black-and-white op-art-style mural design. Slightly larger and more central, the Skate Park Léon Cladel is essentially a purpose-built street spot tucked down an alleyway in the 2nd arrondissement.

Complete with quarterpipe, curbs, and a pyramid, it's ideal for getting to grips with the challenges of street riding without the crowds or dangerous drops.

Finally, EGP 18 (or Espace de Glisse Parisien 18e to give it its full name), in the city's northern reaches, deserves a special mention. The largest covered skatepark in France, it houses 33,000 sq. ft. (3,000 m²) of perfectly smooth concrete and a myriad of features popular with BMXers, skateboarders, rollerbladers, and even freestyle scooter riders.

All of this rich cultural history means that when it comes to Paris hosting the 2024 Olympic Games, the skateboard (street and park) and BMX (freestyle) competitions will blend seamlessly into the fabric of the city. The events take place in a specially created venue on the banks of the Seine in the 18th-century Place de la Concorde, which will also host the breaking and 3×3 basketball competitions—creating a central, if temporary, hub for street-influenced sports on the world stage.

BALLET ON A BMX

*FLATLAND RIDING ON MATTHIAS DANDOIS'S
HOME TURF*

If there's a BMX rider who embodies Paris's crossover of urban sports and artistry, it's Matthias Dandois. Raised on the outskirts of the French capital, he started off riding street before a chance encounter with someone performing flatland tricks—think ballet on a BMX—changed his life forever. Dandois has since become the most dominant flatland rider of his generation, bringing the niche BMX discipline to a mainstream audience with edits including *Tour de Flat* and *Snow Symphony*.

"Every time I'm riding in this museum of a town, it boosts my creativity and I'm a better rider because of the environment," says Dandois. While he trains in a sheltered spot in Porte Pouchet in the city's northern reaches—"It's not very sexy, but not many people pass by, which allows me to focus"—his favorite places to ride and immerse himself in the scene are Bastille, République, and the Ministry of Finance. "The energy in Paris is incredible," he adds. "And with Paris 2024 coming up, you can feel the good vibes in the city."

ALWAYS ALREADY A PL

SKATEBOARDING
AND THE
UNLIMITED
POTENTIAL
OF THE CITY

AY

GROUND

By Konstantin Butz

"Terrain is where you find it."
—Terence Maikels, *Thrasher: Insane Terrain* (Universe Publishing, 2001)

"There is nothing fuckin' cooler than taking over, by force, a plot of land in the middle of a city and fuckin' making it your own," skateboarder and filmmaker Coan "Buddy" Nichols says in the documentary *Grindland* (2022), a film about friendship, skateboarding, and concrete skateparks. Nichols is articulating his unvarnished excitement about Burnside skatepark, one of the most notorious skateboarding spots in the world. Burnside started out with just a few dollops of concrete poured by a group of dedicated skateboarders under a bridge in Portland, Oregon. Where the city had left an abandoned parking lot, the protagonists of *Grindland* detected the perfect weatherproof terrain for radical, unrestricted, and undisturbed skate sessions. Following a dedicated do-it-yourself attitude, they brought cement bag after cement bag to build ever more ramps and transitions, slowly turning the space into the full-on skatepark it is today. "I mean, it's fuckin' punk as shit," says Nichols of the skateboarders' conquest of urban territory, emphasizing the subcultural impact of their autonomous, self-determined, and subversive use of the city.

The renegade vision expressed in the unapologetic lingo of street-smart skate rebels in *Grindland* has been a defining feature of skateboarding ever since kids started using wooden boards with four wheels to explore their neighborhoods in search of excitement and adventure. There are probably no

Pro skater TJ Rogers (opposite) makes Barcelona his playground

"SKATEBOARDERS HAVE NEVER DEPENDED ON THE GOODWILL OF CITY PLANNERS."

two sentences that summarize this more accurately than an observation made by writer Craig Stecyk (under the pseudonym Carlos Izan) in the pages of *SkateBoarder* magazine in 1975: "Two hundred years of American technology had unwittingly created a massive cement playground of unlimited potential. But it was the minds of 11-year-olds that could see that potential."

Not only has Stecyk's quote become a much-cited aphorism within skateboard culture and earned its author legendary status, it can also be read as poignant evidence that skateboarders have never depended on the goodwill of city planners. Just like the skateboarders who built Burnside, the 11-year-olds referred to by Stecyk did not wait for their desires to be anticipated by caring municipalities—they simply launched

themselves into the urban sprawl and made do with what they found. Where construction workers saw a slab of inclined pavement, they saw a concrete wave to be surfed; where pedestrians saw an elevated curbstone, they saw a pristine occasion for a grind; where property-owners saw a steep driveway, they saw a downhill run capable of propelling them to breakneck speeds. Everywhere they looked, they saw a potential playground.

What follows from both examples holds true for skateboarders everywhere and at any time: they find their own ways of reacting to and interacting with the

built environment. As soon as the wheels of a skateboard touch any preexisting surface, they turn the respective terrain into a new, unique, and unanticipated space. Consequently, skateboarders have never been in need of prefabricated and distinguished playgrounds. They are constantly creating spaces of ludic experimentation for themselves. As long-time skateboard scholar Becky Beal

DIY skatepark Bournbrook in Birmingham, U.K., and WJ Skatepark + Urban Plaza in Eugene, Oregon

puts it in her book *Skateboarding: The Ultimate Guide* (2013), "Skateboarding is about navigating and redefining the human-built environment. Thus, skateboarding is a technological and artistic response to urbanization." Most importantly, Beal aligns this redefining and responsive sensibility to a "creative ethos of skateboarding [that] is about

continually finding new places or constructing one's own skate spot."

Embodying a response to urbanization, skateboarding enters into a material dialogue with the city. It engages in a physical conversation that may even benefit from a resonant environment that talks back by presenting itself as inaccessible and unskateable on first view. Almost instinctively, and particularly if the city appears to speak a completely different language, skateboarding finds creative challenges for playful translations in the form of appropriations, adaptations, and redefinitions. "This is a central characteristic of

skateboarding, enacting distinctive new uses and so changing urban terrains," summarizes architectural historian Iain Borden in his book *Skateboarding and the City: A Complete History* (2019). In this way, the evolution of skateboarding even depends on encounters with cities that were not built to be skated; they trigger creativity. The more hermetic the city space presents itself, the greater the challenge for skateboarders to use it for their purposes and the more playful ingenuity they invest in redefining and changing their immediate surroundings.

It is part of the subversive allure of skateboarding—and, as Beal suggests, even part of its very own ethos—to explicitly include the creative appropriation of the city in its performances. In a paper entitled *Skateboarding and the Ecology of Urban Space,* published in

"ALMOST INSTINCTIVELY, SKATEBOARDING FINDS CREATIVE CHALLENGES FOR PLAYFUL TRANSLATIONS IN THE FORM OF APPROPRIATIONS, ADAPTATIONS, AND REDEFINITIONS."

"IN WHATEVER FORM THEY MATERIALIZE, URBAN PLAYGROUNDS ARE CONSTANTLY PRODUCED BY SKATEBOARDERS WHENEVER AND WHEREVER THEY SKATE."

the *Journal of Sport and Social Issues* in 2018, skateboard scholars Brian Glenney and Steve Mull write: "The skateboarder observes his or her urban environment with 'wild' eyes, not unlike a survivalist in nature, tuned to architecture that is hospitable to interaction, thereby rewilding the meaning of different spaces." This perspective not only implies a symbiotic approach that organically interconnects skateboarders with the city but also inherently undermines the original definition of a playground as a determined space for leisure activities and recreation. The "rewilding" impact skateboarders generate with their entry into the urban landscape releases the notion of a playground from any need for official affirmation, detailed planning, or verified standardization. No administrators are required to give their go-ahead. No city governments have to assign and approve available real estate. Skateboarders just create urban playgrounds on the spot. These playgrounds are radically wild: they might include the thrill of being chased by janitors, security guards, or the police; they might cause broken wrists and swollen ankles; they might remain for years as monuments of massive concrete or disappear after the few seconds it takes to ollie down a set of stairs. But in whatever form they materialize, urban playgrounds are constantly produced by skateboarders whenever and wherever they skate; the city is always already a playground, right at their feet.

LONDON CALLING

THE PATCHWORK SPRAWL OF THE U.K. CAPITAL IS THE IDEAL URBAN PLAYGROUND

London has been the beating heart of the U.K.'s urban sports scene for five decades, and its importance in the worlds of skate and BMX shows no signs of diminishing. The city's combination of centuries-old architecture, post-war brutalism, and 21st-century glass-fronted skyscrapers offer boarders and riders a plethora of features while acting as a visually thrilling backdrop.

The capital's most iconic location is the Southbank. World-renowned, this sheltered space on the banks of the Thames has been a key meeting point, community hub, and session spot since the early 1970s. In the Undercroft of the brutalist Queen Elizabeth Hall and Purcell Room performance spaces, the then London County Council architecture department unintentionally created the ultimate concrete playground, complete with a plaza, stair set, banks, and rails that can be ridden year-round. During its colorful history (literally, with almost every inch of the space covered in graffiti and tags), it has faced opposition, threats, and risk of closure from the Southbank Centre. But out of adversity has grown a movement, centered around the campaigning efforts of Long Live Southbank, which has seen the space renovated and the status of the Undercroft secured for future generations of London skaters and BMXers. Today, it is just as much a tourist attraction as any of the city's numerous famous buildings or monuments, with groups of gaping passersby guaranteed.

Other landmarks to have graced the pages of skate and BMX magazines are the Chamberlin, Powell, and Bon-designed Barbican Centre, and Christopher Wren's 17th-century masterpiece, St. Paul's Cathedral. Although polar opposites in architectural style, their respective stair sets and plazas showcase the breadth of options for the city's urban sports athletes.

While London might seem like a confection of concrete and glass without room for even a manual pad, it has somehow managed to carve out space for a number of skateparks. The cult classics are House of Vans (central), Clissold Park (north), Victoria Park (east), Stockwell (south), and BaySixty6 (west), but everywhere across the city, local councils are providing funding to transform old metal halfpipes or unused patches of land into properly planned skateparks for all ages and abilities. When combined with an already robust scene and a collection of supportive parents buoyed by the "Sky Brown effect" (Team GB's skateboarding sensation was 13 when she won bronze at the Tokyo Olympics), London's clay soil is fertile ground for future urban sports stars.

The popularity of these subcultures extends beyond the physical acts of skating and BMXing too. Slam City Skates—Europe's oldest skate shop—has been supplying Londoners with boards, clothing, and accessories since 1986, while no summary is complete without mentioning Palace: the iconic skate brand established in 2009 that is now globally recognized for its tongue-in-cheek streetwear drops.

DIY BIRMINGHAM

*HISTORIC STREET SPOTS AND CUSTOM-BUILT
SKATEPARKS IN THE U.K.'S SECOND-LARGEST CITY*

U.K.'s largest city outside London has a rich skate and BMX history that was founded in the 1980s and '90s on the steps of the old Birmingham Central Library. Designed by local architect John Madin, the library was intended to be the centerpiece of a brutalist, utopian reimagining of post-war Paradise Circus. His grand plans were never fully realized and, despite recent reappraisal and local and national campaigning to save the site, it was demolished to make way for a redeveloped library and mix of stores and offices in the mid 2010s. Although the iconic, harsh concrete building and its surroundings are no more, the West Midlands location has a strong underground scene that continues to flourish, with key attractions including the outdoor Bournbrook DIY skatepark and indoor Creation Skatepark.

That's not to say that Birmingham is solely about skateparks. The city is home to a variety of street spots that have been immortalized in magazine shoots and videos over the years—a recent example is British BMX icon Bas Keep's *More Walls* project. Keep based himself in a warehouse southeast of the city's Chinese Quarter to practice for and dial in his various jumps but also unleashed his legendary wall riding on an unsuspecting Birmingham public. The biggest wall ride of the film is an epic leap from an elevated walkway onto the side of a disused building on Ludgate Hill. Other Birmingham-based spots tackled in the edit include a gap imagined especially for the project in which Keep drops between floors in the parking garage of Selfridges, and a mind-bending plunge from the Smallbrook Queensway bridge to Dudley Street below.

GOTHIC TWIST

URBAN SPORTS IN HISTORIC EDINBURGH

If Edinburgh has been the home of Scottish skating since the 1980s, then Bristo Square has been its beating heart for more than four decades. The square has attracted street skaters and BMXers from across the country ever since these sports' formative years, and even the redevelopment of the site in 2015 couldn't hold them back. Despite aggressive architecture and anti-skate measures, the space is still a hive of activity year-round, echoing to the clattering sound of wheels rolling over paving stones.

The city and its Gothic architecture have been the backdrop for numerous shoots over the years, but easily the most famous is Danny MacAskill's 2009 edit for *Inspired Bicycles.* The video launched MacAskill onto the global stage, amassing almost 40 million views and putting Edinburgh on the BMX map in the process. His follow-up, *Way Back Home,* saw him front-flipping off Edinburgh Castle (with special permission, of course).

The city's longest-running skatepark, Transgression, is an indoors, all-weather (handy in Scotland) park on the ground floor of the Ocean Terminal Shopping Centre in the district of Leith. Designed by Vision Ramps, the site includes a bowl, quarterpipes, and a number of trickable features. To the west lies the concrete jungle of Saughton Skatepark, while in the opposite direction, BMXers can practice their pump-track skills in the shadows of the imposing Salisbury Crags at SKELF Bike Park.

TAKE THE BULL BY THE HORNS

RUNNING RIOT IN THE SKATEPARKS AND PUMP TRACKS OF PAMPLONA

Pamplona might not immediately come to mind as a hotspot for urban sports—not when compared to, say, Barcelona—but the northern Spanish city is nevertheless home to a thriving scene. And while the winters on the outskirts of the Pyrenees can be harsh, that doesn't stop riders from bringing the heat throughout the rest of the year. Internationally famous for the Running of the Bulls which takes place at the Fiesta de San Fermín each July, the Navarre province's capital is also the hometown of another individual who isn't afraid of taking life by the horns: Courage Adams. The Nigeria-born, Pamplona-raised BMX rider discovered the sport at the age of 12 when a friend took him to the city's concrete skatepark, and he has been hooked ever since. Known for his manualing skills—both standard and nose—there isn't a ledge, square, or feature that he hasn't ridden in Pamplona. But it's the city's concrete skatepark that he returns to when home between projects and competitions.

Recently renovated by the architect Daniel Yábar—who has designed plazas and parks across Spain—the Antoniutti Skatepark's sprawling concrete construction includes street features (manual pads, rails), as well as bowls and quarterpipes. The fact that it has dedicated lighting makes it a popular spot even after dark. Just north of the skatepark, on the banks of the river Arga, Pamplona also has a pump track that's a regular spot for skaters and riders.

HALL OF MIRRORS

*RIDING THE REFLECTIVE SURFACES OF PAMPLONA'S
MIRROR PARK WITH COURAGE ADAMS*

The first project that put Courage Adams firmly
on the world stage was 2018's *Mirror Park*.
"My team manager called me and said that
he'd had the idea to do a skatepark made out
of mirrors while brushing his teeth," Adams
says. Planned for six months and shot in just
two days, the film saw Adams and Paul Thölen
ride a fully reflective skatepark that had been
specially built by ramp manufacturers BAAM
on the outskirts of Pamplona.

The 90-second edit was a highlights
reel of Adams's abilities on two wheels, and he
threaded together his signature combinations
of manuals, spins, and grinds like he was an
avatar in a computer game. But the process
of riding on mirrors was more difficult than he
makes it look.

"The hardest part was not knowing
where the ramps were or what they looked
like," he says. "It was super hard to do the lines
and the tricks that you wanted because finding
reference points was so hard."

HOMAGE TO CATALONIA

REVELING IN BARCELONA'S SMORGASBORD OF SPOTS

Arguably Spain's cultural and artistic capital, Barcelona has so many session-able spots that it feels (unintentionally) designed as a skate and BMX playground. Throw in a relaxed attitude toward extreme sports and riders are more likely to attract a crowd of passersby when hitting a spot than be told to move on.

Possibly the best known of all its locations is Fòrum. Situated along the coast across from the main downtown area, the open-air space hosts festivals and concerts but is also home to an iconic wave-like brick quarterpipe and numerous rails and ledges.

Back toward the city center, there's a different feature at every turn. Must-visits include the huge single ledge in front of the modernist-inspired, Richard Meier-designed MACBA, the central Plaça de la Universitat, and the yellow pavement of street spot-turned-skatepark Paral-lel. Parks-wise, Skatepark de Les Corts' concrete plaza and beachside Skatepark de la Mar Bella are tough to beat.

It's not just an abundance of pyramids, ledges, staircases, plazas, and skateparks that make Barcelona such a welcoming space. Even during winter, temperatures remain mild, so it's possible to skate or ride year-round. Plus, the mini ramps at the Sant Jordi Sagrada Familia hostel and the Nevermind bar show how the subculture is firmly ingrained and actively encouraged by the city and its residents.

COMING IN FROM THE COLD

CZECH PRO MAXIM HABANEC RIDES THE MARBLE EXPANSES
OF MOSCOW'S SOVIET-ERA ARCHITECTURE

You have to be tough to skate street in Moscow. Snow and freezing temperatures persist for approximately half the year, and interactions with police can be pretty intense—a hangover from decades of totalitarianism. The history of the USSR continues to cast its long and imposing shadow over Russia, but the architectural legacy is, paradoxically, heaven for skaters: overbearing monuments, grand municipal buildings, and oceans of marble.

"Since we have many great spots at home built by Russia back in the communist period, we thought it would be great to go out there and ride the never-ending marble spots,"

explains Czech pro skater Maxim Habanec. "I couldn't believe how many crazy spots there were in Moscow."

Russia is a land of extremes. Grinding poverty co-exists with the obscene wealth that has fueled a construction boom of glass and steel towers that now make up the Moscow skyline. An eclectic mix of golden-domed Orthodox cathedrals and classical Tsarist architecture; Soviet modernism and neoclassicism; and the queasy glitz of its oligarch-driven transition to hyper-capitalism makes the city a stimulating patchwork to skate. "And if you go in mid-summer," Habanec says, "you also get nice long days and perfect weather."

PUSHING IT TO THE MAX

MAXIM HABANEC GETS ROLLING

Born in Prague, Maxim Habanec started skateboarding when he was six. By age nine he was already in the pages of Europe's biggest skate magazine, and he has maintained this rapid pace of development ever since: whether he's helping to design skateparks in his hometown or teaching skateboarding in India, Habanec is never still. His *Skate of Mind* series was devised as a way to feed his hunger for travel and to explore cities around the world in search of the very best skate spots. Now three series deep, *Skate of Mind* has taken Habanec around the globe several times and given him the chance to skate with the best local talent in each destination. Whether chasing tows from double-decker buses in London, hitting gaps outside Buddhist temples in Bangkok, or cruising along empty desert roads around Dubai and Abu Dhabi, Habanec is happy to launch himself into the local topography.

BOHEMIAN RHAPSODY

PRACTICING URBAN SPORTS IN THE STORIED STREETS OF PRAGUE

The City of a Hundred Spires blends medieval relics with art deco and contemporary architectural gems. Its compact center consists of an old town and new town on either sides of the Vltava river, and visitors can cross between the two via the 15th-century Bohemian sandstone Charles Bridge.

Urban athletes need only turn a corner to be confronted with old squares, stair sets, and lanes ripe for sessioning. But the draw of the city's rich culture at prices much lower than the rest of Europe means central Prague is often crowded with tourists. Fortunately, there are a number of street spots and skateparks on the city's outskirts that can be reached easily using its metro system.

The most iconic street spot in the city has something of a dark history. Located in Letná Park, its grand marble flagstones and ledges were once the base of the world's largest monument to Joseph Stalin (it's still known among locals as Stalin Plaza). Demolished by the Czech government in 1962, it has been the site of alternative culture since the fall of communism, and its skaters and BMXers discovered its smooth surfaces around the same time.

As for more official skateparks, there are at least 10 to choose from in Prague. One of the newest additions can be found by the Vltavská metro station. Situated under a busy bridge, the former pedestrian underpass has been transformed by U/U Studio into an urban sports playground, complete with a bouldering wall and colorful artwork by local skater and artist Jakub Karlík.

RIDE OR DIE

FABIO WIBMER LOOKS BACK ON A SEMINAL VISIT TO PRAGUE WITH STREET TRIALS STAR DANNY MACASKILL

If there are two bike athletes who have transcended the niche discipline of trials riding to become two of the most renowned riders in the world, it's Fabio Wibmer and Danny MacAskill. Every video or new project they release is a guaranteed viral hit as they push themselves, and their sport, to new heights.

Back in 2013, the pair visited Prague with teammate Ali Clarkson as part of an *Inspired Bicycles* edit around the city. "There were lots of places to have fun on any bike," says Wibmer. "In every bigger city, you'll find unique places to ride, but I liked the historical architecture in Prague." The film shows them hopping, pivoting, and tricking their way across the Czech capital in what was one of Wibmer's first video releases. At the time, he was still making a name for himself and considered MacAskill one of his heroes. "His videos inspired me to ride trials," he says. "Nowadays he's still killing it on every bike and I really enjoy watching him ride or having a session with him."

HOW ARCHITECTS
AND DESIGN
FIRMS CAN MAKE
THE CITY MORE
INCLUSIVE FOR
URBAN SPORTS—
AND MORE LIVABLE
FOR EVERYONE

FORMS OF LIBERATION

By Iain Borden

Since the Tokyo Olympics, skateboarding has been firmly established on the world stage. Sky Brown (who won a bronze medal at just 13) is a social media sensation, skate brands like Supreme, Palace, and Vans are household names, and skateboarders worldwide number in the tens of millions. So how does this global success translate into architecture and urban design that helps make cities more inclusive places?

One obvious answer is skateparks—stand-alone facilities tailored to skateboarding, BMX, scooters, and other wheeled activities. After an initial 1970s tranche of commercial skateparks failed to pay back their investors, since 2000 there has been a massive skatepark renaissance, typically charity-run wooden indoor or, more usually, free access city-owned concrete outdoor facilities, ranging from neighborhood affairs to big-budget spectaculars attracting international visitors. One example of the latter is the world's first ever purpose-built multi-story indoor skatepark, F51 in Folkestone, England, which opened in 2022 at a cost of more than £17 million—roughly $21 million.

Designed by Hollaway Studio with Maverick and Cambian, a concrete bowl floor sits below two floors of wooden flow bowl and street course, alongside climbing walls and an Olympic boxing ring. F51 dynamically integrates skate surfaces and architectural form, and also sits within a much larger urban regeneration project. But such big-budget opportunities arise rarely, and spectacular skateparks such as this one need to be supplemented with more street-based spaces. Fortunately, designers have found many alternative ways to integrate skateboarding into cities—here are three of their tactics.

PARKS

At the $4.5 million Paine's Park in Philadelphia, Anthony Bracali and Friday Architects/Planners created a space that was not explicitly skateable. Public meetings fostered shared dialogues between skaters and non-skaters, with Bracali keen to build "something that non-skaters felt that they could support," drawing on desire lines and local topography. New walkways and materials integrate Paine's into its surroundings, and the result, opened in 2013, is a park where people go "not because it's tranquil," according to Bracali, "but for the mix of things that they see and experience." In Tartu, Estonia, TajuRuum used a similar approach for a riverside promenade, incorporating skateable ledges and stairs to integrate urban sports with more leisurely activities. Smaller still, projects such as City Mill Skate (2022) for the UCL East campus in London seek to insert micro "skate dots" amid a larger public landscape to encourage more inclusive visitors and diverse uses.

> # "AFTER AN INITIAL 1970S TRANCHE OF COMMERCIAL SKATEPARKS FAILED TO PAY BACK THEIR INVESTORS, SINCE 2000 THERE HAS BEEN A MASSIVE SKATEPARK RENAISSANCE."

F51 indoor skatepark in Folkestone, U.K., by Hollaway Studio dynamically integrates skate surfaces and architectural form

North of London, Oxhey Activity Park (2020) translates Paine's hard surfaces into a more extended natural landscape. On an elongated site, landscape architects Southern Green interspersed a skate plaza, pump track, snake run, and ramps with dirt trails, soft-play areas, greenery, a cafe, and climbing frames. It's less a skatepark than a wheeled leisure landscape, where urban sports coexist with other activities.

ART
Although moonscape skatepark surfaces form a unique architectural typology, recalling Isamu Noguchi and Nancy Holt sculptures, they are seldom treated as art. Rare exceptions are Koo Jeong A's glow-in-the-dark Otro (2012) on the French island of Vassivière; Evertro (2015) in Everton, England; and OooOoO

(2021), in the shadow of Frank Gehry's Tower at the Parc des Ateliers in Arles, France, all inspired by dripping paint, the wilderness, and Kant's notion of perpetual peace. Similarly enigmatic is Skatepark Continua (2020) at Galleria Continua in Boissy-le-Châtel, France. Beside an old paper mill, and alongside works by Anish Kapoor, Kader Attia, and Antony Gormley, MBL Architectes with David Apheceix formulated a snaking path, whose various contractions, obstacles, and elevations pose multiple riding challenges.

More commonly, skateable art comes as sculptures for riders to

appropriate, including examples by Jeppe Hein, Simparch, and The Side Effects of Urethane. Near Folkestone's F51, multi-disciplinary studio Assemble installed Skating Situations as part of 2021's Folkestone Triennial, now a permanent fixture, with local Kentish ragstone rocks appended by cast steel additions, producing idiosyncratic but highly rideable objects. Assemble's

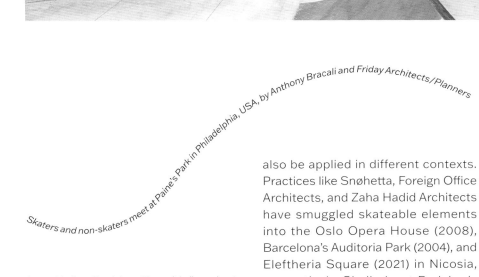

Skaters and non-skaters meet at Paine's Park in Philadelphia, USA, by Anthony Bracali and Friday Architects/Planners

Jane Hall calls this a "humble" project, where skaters become "guardians of the public realm" by simply hanging out, creating social space.

SKATEABLE SPACE

The stealth quality of many of these projects—objects that do not seem to be overtly intended for skateboarding—can also be applied in different contexts. Practices like Snøhetta, Foreign Office Architects, and Zaha Hadid Architects have smuggled skateable elements into the Oslo Opera House (2008), Barcelona's Auditoria Park (2004), and Eleftheria Square (2021) in Nicosia, respectively. Similarly, at Podchody Vltavská in Prague, U/U Studio and artist Jakub Karlík transformed an otherwise barren pedestrian underpass into a multi-colored skate spot in 2021.

Larger landscapes have also been subjected to this quiet approach, including Unity Square (3Deluxe, 2020) in Kaunas, Lithuania, and Landhausplatz (LAAC Architekten and Stiefel Kramer Architecture, 2011) in Innsbruck, Austria. Here undulating banks, ledges, plateaus, and blocks accommodate a new mélange of urban activities for skaters, pedestrians, and BMX-riders alike.

Most recently, a whole skate landscape has emerged at the Nike European HQ in Hilversum, the Netherlands. For HomeCourt (2021), designer Rich Holland of F31, constructors Nine Yards, engineer Bedir Bekar, and sculptor Rubén Sánchez combined dramatic tubes, bumps, ledges, and colorful forms that infuse urban space with sheer irreverent fun. But the backing of a retail giant isn't obligatory: riders themselves have built their own DIY initiatives such as Burnside in Portland, Oregon, and thousands of other examples worldwide, often on wasteland and other disused urban plots.

"THERE IS ALSO THE NEED FOR DESIGNERS AND PLANNERS TO ACCEPT APPLIED USE AND RELINQUISH CONTROL."

Zaha Hadid Architects have smuggled skateable elements into Eleftheria Square in Nicosia, Cyprus

"AT THEIR CORE, SKATEBOARDING AND OTHER URBAN SPORTS CREATIVELY APPROPRIATE RATHER THAN NORMATIVELY UTILIZE CITY SPACES."

What are the lessons of these inventive projects? Most obviously, that skateboarding and urban sports can be inserted into cities in a myriad of different spaces, sizes, and shapes, and that doing so not only brings skateboarding's benefits—independence, confidence, risk-taking, inclusive communities, creativity—into urban spaces but also renders those places more attractive to other users.

But there is also the need for designers and planners to accept applied use and relinquish control. As Bracali advises, "If you've got a strong idea about how it should be used, and it's not being used like that, as it's perfect for something else, you have to think carefully about whether that's a bad

thing." Christos Passas, project director for Zaha Hadid Architects' Eleftheria Square and whose daughter, coincidentally, is a skateboarder, believes that urban spaces should not be designed to be mono-functional: "The minute you start labeling [these spaces], they lose their character a little bit." As for his own work with the firm—which includes the Phaeno Science Center in Wolfsburg, Germany, another site that attracts skateboarders—Passas posits that it's "that sense of making a space more fluid, and curvilinear, that begins to create

new forms of liberation within the urban realm. And I think that's what the athletes like, because they're unrestricted."

At their core, skateboarding and other urban sports creatively appropriate rather than normatively utilize city spaces—a distinction architects and designers working in the urban environment should always respect.

THE GRAND MAZE

*HAZAL NEHIR AND DOMINIC DI TOMMASO CHASE ACROSS
THE ROOFTOPS OF ISTANBUL'S HISTORIC BAZAAR*

Istanbul's Grand Bazaar is a city within a city. Sultan Mehmed the Conqueror ordered its construction in 1455. Over the centuries, it rapidly expanded to reach its current configuration around 1730: a sprawling complex covered in domes and tiled roofs, and comprising a remarkable 64 streets, 22 gates, and more than 3,600 stores. Today, it employs an army of 26,000 workers who serve up to 400,000 customers each day.

Amid its colorful frescoes, marble fountains, and glittering glass lamps, there's a constant hustle and bustle. The Grand Bazaar is a commercial metropolis that belongs to another age and is a radically different world from the concrete, post-war housing estates of suburban Paris that gave birth to parkour in the early 1990s. Still, Turkish freerunner Hazal Nehir had long dreamed of bringing together the modern urban discipline of parkour and the historic elegance of the Grand

Bazaar. "It's such a unique place," she explains. "I have always seen its rooftops in the movies and wanted to jump on them."

Nehir teamed up with Australian freerunner Dominic Di Tommaso and Red Bull, who helped the pair become the first freerunners to gain access to the Grand Bazaar. Nehir and Di Tommaso used the week they were granted to explore every nook and cranny of its 330,000 sq. ft. (30,700 m^2), particularly its famous rooftops, in search of the most creative and challenging parkour lines. The Bazaar's culture and traditions may have changed little over the centuries, but the duo reimagined the landmark as a giant, dynamic labyrinth, naming their resulting film *The Grand Maze*.

Seen from a freerunner's perspective, the hub transforms into something entirely new. As Nehir and Di Tommaso run between the rooftop's ornate metal domes, it looks as though the pair are picking their way through a

lunar landscape littered with boulders. "From its roof, I was fascinated by the atmosphere—it was as if there were no maze-like streets, thousands of shops, and human traffic below us," Nehir reflects. "I had an unforgettable experience in the sky of Istanbul at sunset, accompanied by my friend Dom and the seagulls."

The athletes chose to respond not just to the built environment but interact with the timeless way of life within the Bazaar too. Work carried on as normal throughout the shoot, and the pair improvised with what was around them: weaving through passageways full of shoppers, jumping over rolled carpets carried by porters, and even vaulting over a vendor's back as he leaned down to inspect his wares. Their fusion of parkour and Ottoman-era architecture shows how urban sports can create new possibilities for even the most historic buildings, beyond what their designers could ever have conceived of.

HAZAL NEHIR

TURKEY'S PARKOUR STAR
TRAVERSES ISTANBUL'S
CINEMATIC SKYLINE

Hailing from outside Ankara, Turkey's capital, Hazal Nehir is one of the world's foremost parkour athletes. Nehir has even performed Hollywood stunts and was nominated for a Taurus World Stunt Award in 2020 for her work in Michael Bay's 6 *Underground*.

But at home in Turkey, she struggles to find the necessary challenges and conditions. "It's getting bigger," Nehir says of the country's growing parkour scene. "There aren't too many rails or bars or gyms for training tricks. This affects my training, whereas if you go to Europe, you can find more people better than you, more professional. You can learn more." To aid her progression, Nehir built her own backyard parkour training ground, complete with rails, barriers, and crash mats.

She has often looked enviously at Turkey's historic buildings, including Istanbul's Grand Bazaar, which is usually off-limits to freerunners. Like Nehir, the Grand Bazaar has its own Hollywood credit: Daniel Craig as James Bond drove across its iconic rooftops on motorbike in 2012's *Skyfall*, aided by around 400 technicians. When Nehir finally got her chance to explore the Bazaar's rooftops, she had a more modest, five-person film crew, but the outcome is just as breathtaking.

PERSIAN PASSION

IN TEHRAN, SKATEBOARDING BUILDS BRIDGES, CEMENTS COMMUNITY, AND BREAKS DOWN MISCONCEPTIONS

Outsiders often view Iran with a sense of mystery and profound misunderstanding. Is it safe? Are foreigners allowed to visit? Despite a long-running feud between Iran and the United States—a complicated history that dates back to the 1979 Islamic Revolution and beyond—day-to-day life in Iran is comparatively normal. Major cities like the capital, Tehran, as well as Isfahan and Shiraz have a cosmopolitan culture and boast an enticing architectural mix of ancient Persian and modern Islamic influences, with just about everything in between.

Religious doctrine, Sharia law, and conservative social customs are a feature of the Islamic Republic of Iran. Authorities tend to be less than accommodating of youth culture, particularly subcultures such as skateboarding or rock music that are seen to have deeply American DNA. Yet the reality of experience on the streets is often quite different. Iran has a thriving underground culture: music, art, raves, illegal street races, and even young Iranians

hitchhiking and couch-surfing to travel the country off the beaten track. Iran's skate scene is small but lively and made up of dedicated, passionate riders. There are a few skateparks and skate shops around the country, although harsh sanctions make importing gear and materials tricky—locally pressed boards are made from pine, not the gold standard you find elsewhere: Canadian maple.

In 2017, Red Bull sent an international pro crew to join homegrown skaters in exploring the rich variety of spots Tehran has to offer. Among them were Jaakko Ojanen from Finland, Nassim Lachhab from Morocco, and Carlos Cardeñosa from Spain. All were pleasantly surprised at the positive reception they received and were rarely kicked off spots. In fact, security guards were more often intrigued than incensed by their presence—one even wanted to give skating a go himself, with predictably embarrassing consequences.

Many of Tehran's most popular spots are the kinds found elsewhere in the world: parks, plazas, and shopping

malls. But there are some you could find only in Iran. The Azadi Tower, or "Freedom Tower," is a 150-ft. (45-m) marble-clad masterpiece completed in 1971 that marks the western entrance to Tehran. It was commissioned by the last Shah of Iran, Mohammad Reza Pahlavi, to commemorate 2,500 years of the Persian Empire. A more macabre monument is located across town in the Behesht-e Zahra (Paradise of Zahra) cemetery outside the gold-domed Mausoleum of Ruhollah Khomeini: a long fountain that flows red to symbolize the blood of the martyrs who died fighting in the horrific 1980–1988 Iran-Iraq war, which killed over a million people.

Ojanen, Lachhab, and Cardeñosa joined a gang of local skaters to take on the Grand Bazaar, whose oldest buildings date from the 17th century. The joy they felt while cruising together around its labyrinthine alleyways after the market had closed for the day serves as a powerful reminder that while politics, religion, and nations can divide, skateboarding can unite.

ARCHITECT'S PLAYGROUND

SKATING THE SLEEK SURFACES OF DUBAI

The towering skyscrapers and manicured landscaping of the best-known emirate might seem too pristine for the cut and thrust of urban sports, but Dubai has become a must-visit destination for professional athletes over the last decade.

From 2015's feature-length *We Are Blood* skate film to the Kriss Kyle 2019 *Dropping in on Dubai* edit that saw him jump from a chopper onto the helipad of the Tom Wright-designed Burj Al Arab hotel, the city and its surrounding desert provide a striking contrast to the sprawling bustle of Europe.

Down on terra firma, some of the most sessioned spots are the quarterpipe-like features outside the Dubai Mall. Although street riding in public spaces is technically banned in the city, Dubai's authorities have welcomed Western athletes with open arms, providing permits and access to transform the lavish architecture into an urban sports playground.

The Memorial Fountain at Union Square is another spot that attracts skaters thanks to its super-smooth marble surface and relaxed attitude—members of the public are more likely to sit back and watch the action than call the police.

As with its architecture, Dubai is home to a collection of turbo-charged skateparks to rival any other facility in the world. The biggest and best is the XDubai Skatepark at Kite Beach. Designed by Convic, the 34,500-sq.-ft. (3,200-m^2) site has everything you could want from a skatepark—from miniramps for those just getting started, to fullpipes for the pros.

TAG-TEAMING IN DUBAI

IN THE (SPECIAL ECONOMIC) ZONE WITH
COURAGE ADAMS AND MADARS APSE

The Nigeria-born, Spain-raised BMX athlete Courage Adams is famed for his ability to perform trick combinations straight out of a computer game. A master of street and park riding, his edits and competition runs are the stuff of legend, while his balancing ability when manualing and nose manualing needs to be seen to be believed.

After finally securing his Spanish visa, Adams has been able to travel the world more easily, and in 2020 one of his first stops was Dubai for the film *The Lunch Break.* Shot at various spots around the Dubai International Finance Centre, the video shows Adams and skateboarder Madars Apse tag-teaming gaps, stair sets, and ledges as they evade a security guard.

"It was totally different to anywhere I've ridden before," says Adams. "There are some cool buildings, but if you look for other sites there's nothing, whereas in Europe there are always more spots. The scene is growing though. They have a new skatepark and the locals are already at a good level. I think Dubai is going to be a country with good riders and a good reputation."

TAKING THE

RE

HOW URBAN
ATHLETES
APPROPRIATE
CITY SPACES
TO CREATE NEW
POSSIBILITIES

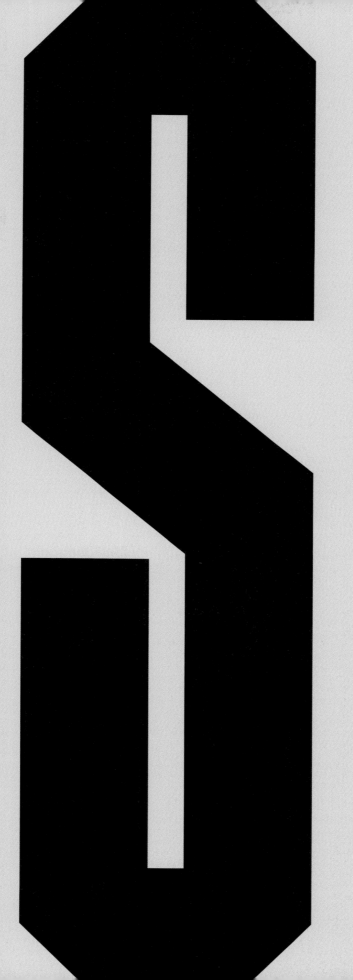

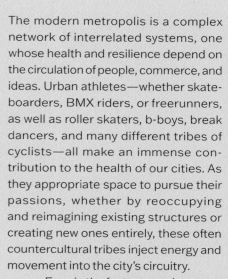

By Alex King

The modern metropolis is a complex network of interrelated systems, one whose health and resilience depend on the circulation of people, commerce, and ideas. Urban athletes—whether skateboarders, BMX riders, or freerunners, as well as roller skaters, b-boys, break dancers, and many different tribes of cyclists—all make an immense contribution to the health of our cities. As they appropriate space to pursue their passions, whether by reoccupying and reimagining existing structures or creating new ones entirely, these often countercultural tribes inject energy and movement into the city's circuitry.

Even in the fastest growing, most prosperous, and best-planned cities, there are neglected areas: post-industrial zones, new developments that struggle to attract much human activity, or in-between spaces with no prescribed use. Urban athletes are a revitalizing force, because they see the city differently to governments, businesses, and everyday citizens. When they look at buildings, streets, and spaces around them, they don't assess their worth based on economic utility, productive capacity, real-estate value, or even beauty. Urban athletes look for possibilities that others don't see. Because they are rarely given appropriate space and infrastructure, instead they have to take it or create it for themselves, happily looking past the problems that discourage others.

British skaters took over the covered area under the brutalist Southbank Centre in London as early as 1973

" URBAN SPORTS CAN INTRODUCE VITAL LIFEBLOOD INTO EVEN THE MOST DEGRADED AND SEEMINGLY HOPELESS URBAN CONTEXTS."

The reconquest of space reinvigorates urban flow in neglected areas all over the world, whatever their context. This energy often seeps out to surrounding areas, providing benefits not just to the original community of urban athletes but to all citizens. Such transformational interventions can happen right in the beating heart of major cities, as much as in the overlooked margins. London's Southbank Centre is perhaps the most famous example. Although it's hard to imagine now, for decades this area on the south-side of the River Thames— originally created as part of the Festival of Britain in 1951 and subsequently developed into a complex of grand brutalist buildings—failed to encourage Londoners to spend time there. The first skateboarders arrived as early as 1973 and took over a covered area full of concrete banks, which became known as

"the Undercroft," and helped foster the emergence of British skateboarding. This vibrant, graffiti-covered zone was finally protected from major redevelopment in 2014 after the hard-fought Long Live Southbank campaign, led by skaters themselves. As a result, the area is still in regular use today.

Urban sports can introduce vital lifeblood into even the most degraded and seemingly hopeless urban contexts. Freerunners Mohammed Aljakhabir and Ahmad Matar were inspired to practice parkour after watching a video of the sport on YouTube while they were in the Khan Yunis refugee camp in Gaza 15 years ago. Galvanized, they began

to envision the concrete shells of destroyed buildings and hulking piles of rubble around them as obstacles to be overcome, and to imagine opportunities to find the most creative routes through the destroyed urban landscape. A community has since blossomed in Gaza, and freerunning provides a much-needed outlet for self-expression and escape.

Matar's dream of developing freerunning infrastructure in Gaza blossomed into the Wallrunners NGO,

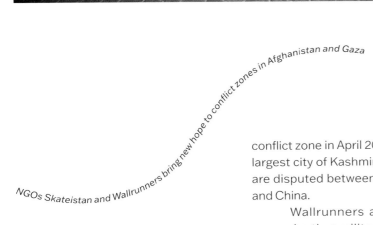

NGOs Skateistan and Wallrunners bring new hope to conflict zones in Afghanistan and Gaza

which puts freerunning at the heart of an ambitious educational program to promote self-growth, build self-esteem, and support positive psychosocial development among young Palestinian girls and boys. Wallrunners successfully crowdfunded to build Gaza's first parkour academy, which opened in December 2020. After demonstrating the transformative effect of parkour in Gaza, Wallrunners expanded to another

conflict zone in April 2021: Srinagar, the largest city of Kashmir, whose borders are disputed between India, Pakistan, and China.

Wallrunners attendees grow up navigating military checkpoints, harassment by soldiers, an intermittent electricity supply, and few life opportunities, which has led to soaring levels of depression among local young people. But when young Kashmiri girls and boys come to Wallrunners to practice parkour and martial arts, they learn to see the potential for movement and creativity in the challenging environment around them, while using art and exercise to heal trauma. Wallrunners is in the

process of opening another center for marginalized youth in Mombasa, Kenya and also has plans for one in Sweden, where Matar now lives.

Urban athletes don't just reimagine existing contexts and structures: they often create entirely new ones of their own. Today, commercial or state-funded skateparks can be found in cities around the world, but the most radically transformative force urban athletes unleash is DIY, or do-it-yourself. DIY can be as simple as putting a sheet of wood or a bit of concrete down as a kicker to help clear a gap on a BMX, or extend to sprawling DIY skateparks.

In 2010, a group of skaters in Tampere, a post-industrial city in southern Finland, began building a skatepark in the ruins of an old matchstick factory, which they christened Tikkutehdas. When the park came under threat of

"IN TRANSFORMING THE CITY, URBAN ATHLETES ARE A SIGNIFICANT, VALUABLE, AND ENERGIZING ELEMENT IN THE URBAN FABRIC."

demolition, they formed an official association, Kaarikoirat (which translates to "Ramp Dogs"), to help them fight to save what they had built.

Kaarikoirat failed to save Tikkutehdas from redevelopment but succeeded in opening a dialogue with the municipality. Kaarikoirat was given permission to build ramps and skateable obstacles in a number of problem spots around Tampere, which they helped revitalize and turn into new social spaces at virtually no cost to the city. The trust they developed led to Kaarikoirat providing input for the construction of the biggest outdoor concrete skatepark in Finland, Iso-Vilunen, in 2015. A year later, they were given a disused pulp mill next to Lake Näsijärvi and transformed it into an enormous indoor concrete bowl, Kenneli DIY, and a lively events and social center, supported by city funding. In the fall of 2021, Kaarikoirat and the City of Tampere made history when they opened the first public high school in the Nordic countries with a specialized skateboarding and communications curriculum—a shining example of what cities can achieve if they work with skateboarders.

Located in Selly Oak in Birmingham, Bournbrook skatepark also made history by becoming the first DIY skatepark to be officially certified in the United Kingdom. Neglected for decades, this small corner of parkland had become overgrown, strewn with waste, and known as "mugger's alley." Local skater Shaun Boyle began clearing the area and was soon joined by an army of volunteers who worked to build a professional-grade skatepark on a shoestring budget. The skaters also planted flowers and small trees and initiated an ongoing dialogue with the local community and council.

The build became a lifeline for many local young people struggling through the first lockdown of the

Covid-19 pandemic. Early on, the project integrated self-determination theory and mental-health awareness, giving young volunteers a sense of purpose and belonging, creating an open space to talk about mental health, and offering a first point of contact for people dealing with self-harm or substance issues.

"We have managed to open a skatepark built for the people, by the people," explains Berni Good, one of the project's directors. "From the beginning we realized the positive impact on the psychological well-being and general health of all involved. The park has overcome the disconnect between what authorities can—or can't—provide and what young people really need."

The creativity unleashed by this endeavor has been felt keenly by the wider community, many of whom have said they felt safe walking through

Bournbrook in Birmingham became the first DIY skatepark to be officially certified in the United Kingdom

the area for the first time. Yet despite almost unanimous community support, Bournbrook skatepark is at risk of being demolished to make space for a supermarket expansion.

It is clear that those cities that recognize the contribution and welcome the participation of urban athletes will be the kinds of cities people will want to live in in future. "Embracing DIY urbanism could play a significant role in giving cities an edge," says Timo Hämäläinen, an independent urban policy advisor who advocates for smarter urban planning in Helsinki and worldwide. "Bureaucratic, siloed structures are a relatively recent development—historically, cities

built with a very organic, DIY practice have been successful and sustainable over time."

Wherever you live and however challenging the context, skateboarders, BMX riders, and freerunners' interventions in public space make the environment healthier and more vibrant for all. In transforming the city, urban athletes are a significant, valuable, and energizing element in the urban fabric.

TWO WORLDS

*HOW THE BMX SCENES DIFFER IN
THE MEGACITIES OF TOKYO AND OSAKA*

The two Japanese megacities of Tokyo and Osaka are, at first glance, very similar. Both are among the most densely populated cities in Japan, despite Tokyo ranking first with over three times the population of Osaka. Both are considered to be among the most livable cities in the world and bicycles are an important means of urban transportation in both, albeit highly regulated. For BMX fans, the only place to work on skills is almost exclusively at designated skate-parks. Prominent in Tokyo are the Murasaki Sports Park, located north of the city center and, close to the sea, the Jonanjima Skate Park, while in the wider Osaka Prefecture, BMX courses can be found in Oizumi Ryokuchi Park and in Kishiwada.

But there are subtle differences between the two ostensibly very similar cities, located only about 300 miles (500 km) apart, that are reflected in their urban sports scenes. Shibuya, Harajuku, and the Musashino areas are among the most popular BMX spots in Tokyo, but the community in the Japanese capital is subdivided from district to district and somewhat detached. By contrast, the scene in Osaka is smaller but much more tightly knit and arguably more open-minded and laid-back: its BMX scene is internationally renowned for being a fun and dedicated crew. The absolute superstar of the region is BMX freestyle rider Rim Nakamura, who represented Japan at the Summer Olympics in Tokyo in 2021, finishing fifth in the BMX freestyle competition.

METROPOLIS OF MINARETS

DOMINIC DI TOMMASO'S VERSATILITY IS PUT TO THE TEST BY CAIRO'S MIX OF MODERN, HISTORIC, AND ANCIENT ARCHITECTURE

The city of a thousand minarets, Cairo is the biggest urban agglomeration in the Arab world and the center of the region's political and cultural life. The richness and variety of its Islamic architecture is world-renowned, and a key reason Australian freerunner Dominic Di Tommaso was lured there for a freestyle dash across the baking-hot capital in 2019.

His first stop, the Salah El-Din Citadel, was originally built in the late 12th century and was the residence of Egypt's ruling dynasties for nearly 700 years. The citadel's commanding position in the Mokkatam Hills provided Di Tommaso with the perfect vantage point for surveying the countless minarets rising from mosques across the city below.

Cairo has swelled to encompass the ancient Egyptian cities of Heliopolis, Memphis, and Giza—the latter includes the Giza pyramid complex, Di Tommaso's final destination. But first he had to navigate the chaotic rooftops of the modern Nazlet El-Semman neighborhood, adjacent to the Sphinx. Nearby, the three pyramids were built roughly between 2550 and 2490 BCE, the secrets of their immense construction still hotly debated by archaeologists. But whether he's vaulting across modern concrete rooftops or ancient monuments that have sweltered under the Egyptian sun for millennia, it's all in a day's work for Di Tommaso.

STREET THEATER

BUILDING A BMX SCENE IN BUSY LAGOS

Lagos is a cultural powerhouse. From fashion to food, film, and music, the Nigerian city is humming with creativity. But in the largest metropolitan area in Africa—home to 23.5 million people and among the fastest growing cities in the world—space is constantly being negotiated.

Until recently, there was no BMX scene in Lagos. But all that changed when the Lagos BMX Crew came together, determined to make their presence felt on the cultural stage and carve out a bright future for the sport in Nigeria.

Led by a mechanic named Starboy, the crew faced an uphill battle to build a BMX community in a city with no infrastructure for urban sports. Its first and only skate shop opened in 2017 and, to date, there are no BMX stores and no skateparks—Lagos might just be the biggest city in the world without either.

Starboy found his BMX at a market stall selling kids' toys and began teaching himself tricks by watching YouTube videos on his phone. Today, he learns from the streets: "They're the best teachers," he says. Starboy found kindred spirits in riders KK Money, a schoolteacher by day, and S-King, who hails from Makoko, an informal settlement known as the "Venice of Lagos" that floats on the lagoon in the shadow of the seven-mile (11-km) Third Mainland Bridge. Riding together has filled their lives with positivity, inspiration, and abundant creativity.

To stand out against the frenetic energy of the city, riders in Lagos need to make a big impression. With no support structure or older riders to look up to, Lagos's first generation of BMX stars are forced to be innovative. Here, riders can't hide away in parks, perfecting tricks for hours: BMX is an entirely public affair. Riders in Lagos are not just athletes, they're performers too—and when the guys get together it feels more like a pedaling street circus than your average BMX jam. They quickly draw large crowds, wowing audiences with flatland tricks, acrobatics, and daring jumps, playing off each other and sometimes even involving the crowd in the action.

Starboy, S-King, and KK Money have a gift for entertaining, and are always looking for new ways to interact with the city around them and its inhabitants. But using the streets as their stage is about more than necessity or putting on a show: they are planting the seeds for the next generation of riders to grow and flourish. Building, developing, and sustaining a thriving BMX scene in Lagos is a challenge, but the BMX Crew are in for the long haul. "If you fall [off a horse], you must surely climb back on," explains KK Money, translating a common Yoruba saying into English. "Continue, you must surely conquer it. Once you get it right, it's forever."

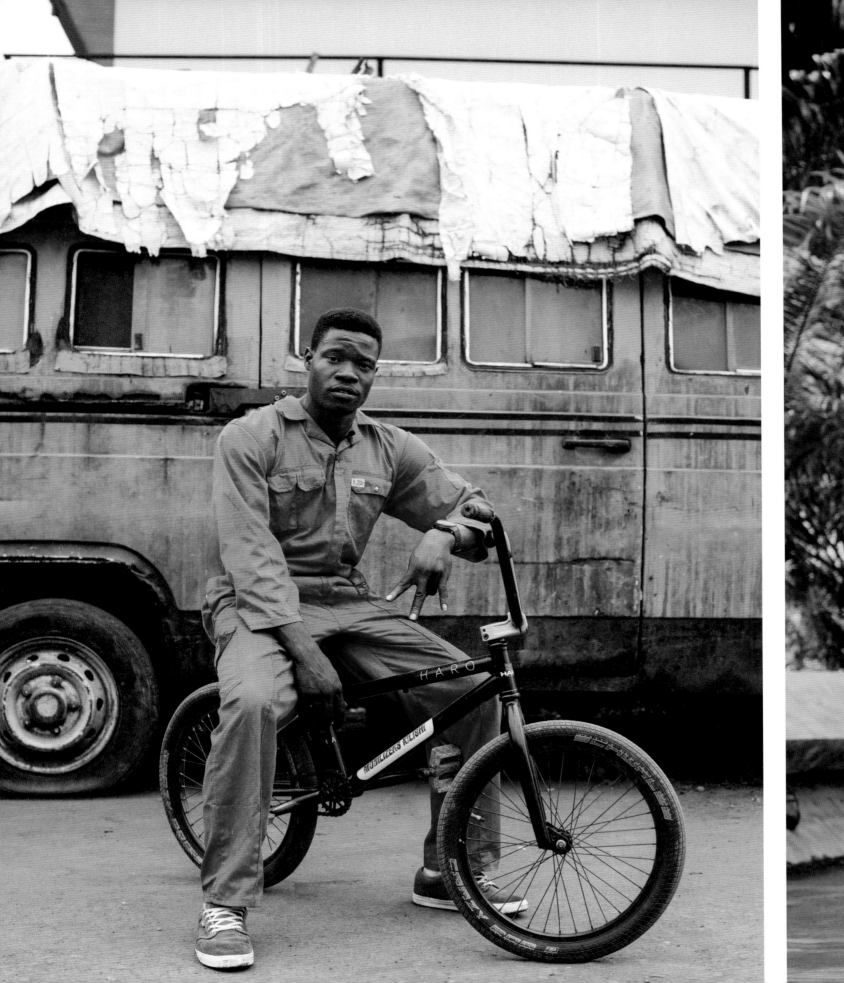

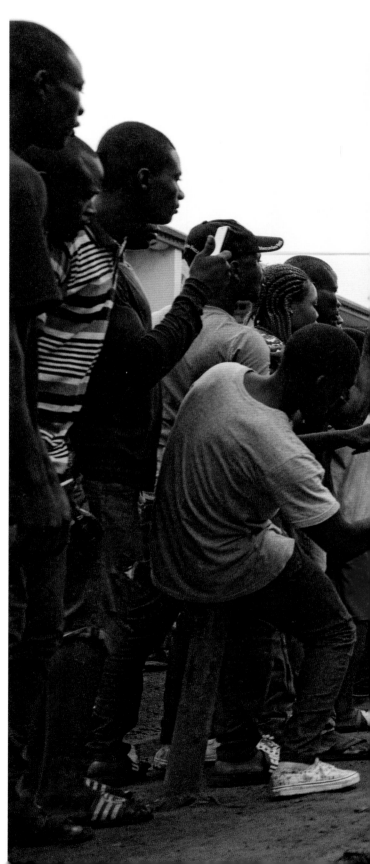

FALLING AND GETTING BACK UP AGAIN

A SKATEPARK IN A KAMPALA TOWNSHIP GIVES CHILDREN AND TEENAGERS NEW HOPE

Nonprofit organization skate-aid provides comprehensive child and youth services through the educational power of skateboarding. Since its founding in 2009 by German skateboarding pioneer Titus Dittmann, it has implemented more than 25 projects in 19 countries worldwide, with a special focus on Africa, including skatepark projects in Namibia, Uganda, Mozambique, Tanzania, Kenya, and South Africa.

Projects are carried out with local partners, such as SOS Children's Villages, the Associação do Skate de Moçambique, Don Bosco Mondo, the Global Experience, and the Goethe-Institut. The aim throughout has been to provide these local partners with support until they are able to operate on their own. Among other things, skate-aid assists with the implementation of educational skateboarding workshops, the training of local volunteers as skateboard coaches, and organization.

The nonprofit's skatepark in Kampala has been particularly successful: running since 2010 in cooperation with the Uganda Skateboard Union and its president Jack Mubiru, the park in Kitintale Township, which has a population of around 20,000, has expanded and improved continuously since opening, and plans are in place to gradually develop the park into a fully fledged youth center.

SKATE-AID

*SKATEBOARDING HELPS TO FOSTER
AUTONOMY IN KIDS*

For skate-aid, skateparks and skateboards are
vital tools for the long-term empowerment of
children and adolescents. Their main mission
is to provide kids with developmental support,
especially in places where social grievances
and difficult living conditions prevail, such
as in Uganda, Namibia, Syria, Palestine, and
Nepal. In doing so, the organization provides
guidance, contributes to gender equality, and
helps to raise self-esteem.

This strengthens motivation, community awareness, personal responsibility, and
determination over the long term. Put simply,
when kids get back up again on their own after
falling down, they learn not to be afraid and
also to embrace new challenges throughout
their lives. Thanks to the efforts of skate-aid,
children and adolescents grow into strong,
self-determined individuals who enrich their
communities—especially in places with un-
favorable living conditions and a lack of hope
and perspective.

CREATIVE ALCHEMY

BMX PRO COURAGE ADAMS HAS HIS EYES OPENED AND HIS MIND BLOWN BY THE CREATIVITY ON THE STREETS OF SOWETO

If you're running low on inspiration, Johannesburg is the city for a full recharge—an overload, even. When Spanish BMX pro Courage Adams arrived to check out the best spots in Jozi, as locals call Johannesburg, he was immediately taken by its energy. "I felt really connected with the city," says Adams, who was born in Benin City, Nigeria, before moving to Spain. "The local culture reminds me of when I was a kid in Nigeria."

The Jozi BMX scene is increasingly strong. Downtown boasts striking architecture and public artworks, giving riders of all levels plenty of challenges, as well as the building blocks to piece together jaw-dropping lines. Across town, Soweto—with its powerful history of oppression and resistance—continues to be central to South African cultural output, from fashion and hip hop to jazz and ultra-high-tempo dance music. The skateparks here might not be at the level to which Adams is accustomed, but Sowetans don't let limitations get in their way. The atmosphere alone is electric.

Thando Montangane is a BMX spinner who welded two BMXes together in his own two-wheeled twist on Soweto's now-world-famous spinning subculture—where drivers throw their cars in circles at high speeds, performing stunts inside and outside of the car while throwing up thick clouds of tire smoke. Like many before him, Adams left impressed by the cultural alchemy of Soweto, where people constantly invent new and beautiful creations from next-to-nothing.

LEAP FOR GOLD

*FREERUNNER DOMINIC DI TOMMASO ON
NEW, CREATIVE WAYS TO MOVE THROUGH
JOHANNESBURG'S ARCHITECTURAL TREASURES*

With its long gold-mining heritage, Johannesburg is also known as "Egoli," or "The City of Gold." In his own way, Australian free-runner Dominic Di Tommaso has been searching for gold throughout his career too, looking at cities and finding their particular, hidden treasures.

Di Tommaso came to freerunning in 2007 via an unorthodox route: growing up he was into dance, ballet, and figure skating but went on to work full-time as a garbage collector. This range of influences and experiences could explain the fresh approach he brings to each new challenge. The athlete has risen to the very top because he finds the golden opportunities—the gaps, the lines, the trick potential—that others don't, in the streets, buildings, and landscape of a city.

In Johannesburg, Di Tommaso found rich pickings in the city's architectural gems: Soweto Theatre, Gold Reef City amusement park, Hillbrow's iconic Ponte Tower, and Sandton's gleaming financial district. "I loved the uniqueness of each location," he says, "and how its architecture is informed by its culture and its past—as well as its present."

FINDING RELEASE IN CAPE TOWN

SKATERS AND BMXERS HUSTLE TO CONTINUE DOING WHAT THEY LOVE

Fewer cities boast such awe-inspiring topography as Cape Town. The South African port city lies in the shadow of the mighty Table Mountain and juts out into the South Atlantic Ocean, just hours from the southernmost point on the entire African continent. From the city's northern coast, you can see Robben Island, the notorious spot where Nelson Mandela was imprisoned for 18 years.

The ocean, hills, and mountains that surround the city make a spectacular backdrop for skate and BMX edits, but while South Africans have been skating since the 1960s, there's not much in the way of dedicated infrastructure. The city's BMX riders and skateboarders realized long ago that nobody was going to hand them anything, and this has fueled a strong DIY ethos that makes Cape Town one of the most exciting urban sports cities in the country.

South Africa is a surfer's country, producing household names such as Shaun Tomson, Jordy Smith, and Cape Town's own WSL rising star Michael February. While these figures rake in global endorsements, skaters and BMX riders have to make do with scraps from the table. Since skateboarding became an Olympic sport, the government has started to invest in small skateparks across the country, but in Cape Town, local spots are pretty gritty and sometimes even dangerous. Still, while BMXes and boards are prohibitively expensive for many kids, the hills are free—as is ecstatic hill bombing.

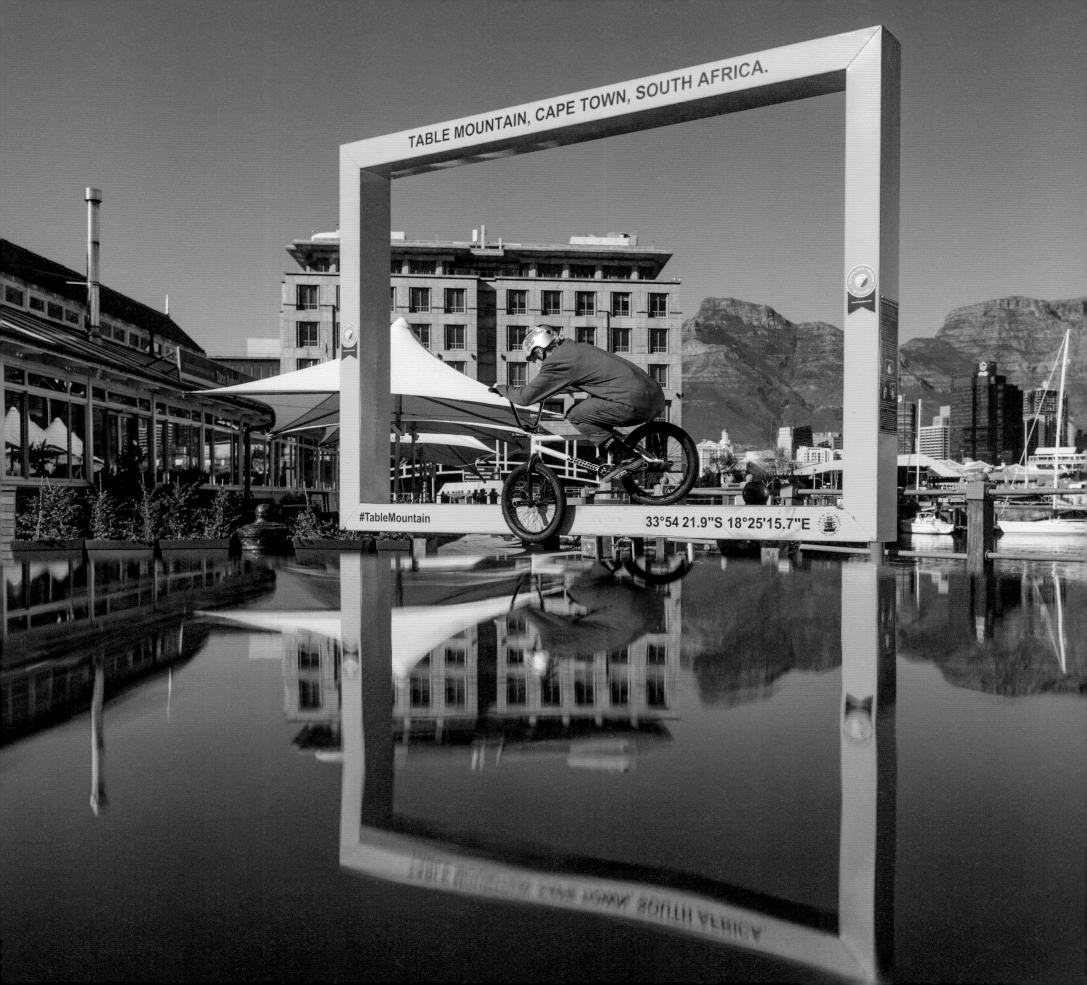

SHAPES IN THE CITY

MURRAY LOUBSER PROVES HIS ARCHITECTURE AND BMX BONAFIDES IN A THRILLING FILM

Though born in Cape Town, Murray Loubser left the city with his family for the scenic coastal village of Gansbaai in Western Cape when he was in his teens. Gansbaai is a destination for whale-watchers but not so much for BMX riders. So, when Loubser started to ride BMX at 16, he had to build his own jumps on a piece of scrubland near his parents' house. Without the usual BMX spots and riders' hangouts, Loubser's talent developed organically, along with an intuitive, creative approach to riding. Much later, when Loubser joined the BMX circuit, his distinctive riding style drew attention, along with a reputation for being one of the most innovative BMX street riders in South Africa.

Shapes in the City is a project celebrating the unique forms and surreal shapes of urban architecture. Co-created with photographer Wayne Reiche, Loubser gives viewers the opportunity to see the city through the eyes of a BMX rider: spotting the lines, gaps, transitions, and shapes that people typically look past each day, but which lend themselves to spectacular runs. Released in 2020, the project began as a photographic series but soon developed into a film that pushes at the aesthetic and intellectual limits of BMX filmmaking.

SMELLS
LIKE

WHO ACTUALLY
INVENTED THE
SPORTS THAT HAVE
BEEN CHANGING
THE FACE OF OUR
CITIES FOR THE
PAST 50 YEARS?
A FORAY INTO THE
EARLY DAYS OF BMX,
SKATEBOARDING,
AND PARKOUR

N SPIRIT

By Andreas Wollinger

Only a handful of people might recognize the name Scot Alexander Breithaupt, and yet he has, arguably, changed the world. Born in Long Beach, a community on the outskirts of Los Angeles, California, Breithaupt is considered the Godfather of BMX. By the age of 13, he had, if not invented, then at least shaped and made great this unique form of biking.

The year was 1970, and Breithaupt and his friends dreamed of motocross bikes. They naturally couldn't afford these off-road motorcycles, so instead they modified their bicycles by adding wide motorcycle handlebars, smaller knobby tires, reinforced frames, and,

most importantly, a round metal plate for attaching a race number to the front.

The group began to hone their riding skills at a vacant lot in Long Beach. Breithaupt founded the Bicycle United Motocross Society (BUMS), wrote a rulebook including a point system, and defined the difficulty levels of various jumps and stunts—a prerequisite for holding the first California BMX Championship in 1972. The first world championships were held just 15 years later, and BMX has been an Olympic sport since 2008. BMX racing made its debut at the Beijing Olympics, and a free-style event was added in Tokyo in 2020.

Breithaupt's story is a perfect example of the way underground sports emerged in the second half of the 20th century: teenagers, blessed with an irrepressible love of life, playful creativity, and youthful abandon, created activities off the cuff that had previously been considered impossible—and looked outrageously good doing them. Although this kind of urban expression

169

BMX bikers Bruno Hoffmann and Danny MacAskill on the Teufelsberg in Berlin and Calton Hill in Edinburgh

"TEENAGERS, CREATED ACTIVITIES OFF THE CUFF THAT HAD PREVIOUSLY BEEN CONSIDERED IMPOSSIBLE."

has almost always been a nuisance for the adult world at first, that has done nothing to diminish the popularity and cool factor of the activity in question—quite the contrary, in fact. Under ideal circumstances, a subculture develops as a result of this excitement, combined with a whole new attitude to life that is accompanied by its own fashions and magazines.

Skateboarding was no different, though it took much longer to develop. It was invented in Southern California in the 1950s by a few surfers who had grown bored waiting for the perfect waves. They mounted metal wheels from roller skates (initially without ball bearings) on small boards similar in shape to surfboards and referred to the sport as "sidewalk surfing" because it imitated the motion of surfing on beachfront sidewalks.

The first skateboarding magazines appeared in the mid-1960s. Because skateboarding was banned on public streets, aficionados looked for alternative playgrounds, which they found in empty California swimming pools shaped like bathtubs with rounded sides. (It has been suggested that Alvar Aalto's kidney-shaped pool at the Villa Mairea in Finland provided the inspiration for those same California pools that attracted early skateboarders.) And these pools were the precursor of the halfpipe, giving skateboarders a new direction: vertical. They soon learned that if they were able to ride up the walls

with enough momentum, they could make aerial jumps and use that skill to develop acrobatic tricks.

It would take another decade for two events to give skateboarding another boost. The first was the replacement of metal wheels by those made of polyurethane, which increased grip and—thanks also to the use of ball bearings—made higher speeds possible.

The curved lines of an L.A. skatepark and Oscar Niemeyer's museum inspire Letícia Bufoni, Pedro Barros, and Murilo Peres

The second happened in 1976, when 13-year-old Alan "Ollie" Gelfand invented a trick that would become the foundation of street skating: the "ollie." Christened after Gelfand's nickname, the technique allows rider and board to leap into the air without the use of the rider's hands, enabling skateboarders to negotiate obstacles.

In the mid-1980s, another teenager emerged as a shining role model for the sport: Californian Tony Hawk. Hawk was world champion 12 years in a row, developed more than 80 new tricks, and in 1999 became the first person to land a 900, a trick involving the completion of two-and-a-half mid-air revolutions in the halfpipe. In Hawk's wake, the subculture flourished worldwide, and skateparks sprang up everywhere. Enthusiasm for skateboarding remains strong to this day, and Hawk, now in his mid-fifties, has a highly successful video game series that bears his name.

In 1989, in the Parisian suburb of Lisses, 16-year-old David Belle created what was by far the most exciting method of getting around a city: parkour. The aim of this discipline is to use only the capabilities of your own body to overcome all obstacles in your path, as elegantly and fluidly as possible. It sometimes seems as if parkour practitioners, called *traceurs*, effortlessly suspend the laws of physics as they make their way from point A to point B—when they scale meter-high walls, land and balance on ledges and railings the width of a hand, or jump from one house to another, unfazed by dizzying differences in height. But the concept is older than it seems—the idea had been around for nearly 100 years by the time parkour was invented. In the early 20th century, French military

"UNDER IDEAL CIRCUMSTANCES, A SUBCULTURE DEVELOPS AS A RESULT OF THIS EXCITEMENT, COMBINED WITH A WHOLE NEW ATTITUDE TO LIFE."

"ALL THREE SPORTS MAY HAVE THEIR OWN UNIQUE HISTORIES, BUT THEY HAVE PERMANENTLY CHANGED OUR PERSPECTIVE OF THE URBAN ENVIRONMENT."

officer Georges Hébert created a training method, *la méthode naturelle,* that combined various forms of human movement and the natural environment. Sixty years later, soldiers in the Indochina Wars used his techniques to escape more quickly and efficiently in the jungle. Raymond Belle, David's father, was born in Vietnam in 1939 and passed his knowledge on to his son, who eventually translated the technique to the urban jungle.

In the early 21st century, Frenchman Sébastien Foucan refined the rather straightforward and decidedly purist form of parkour movement to create freerunning, a discipline that looks even more spectacular and incorporates all kinds of acrobatic elements. Freerunning is less about efficiency in moving from point A to B than it is focused on the elegance with which you are able to

Freerunners Hazal Nehir and Dominic Di Tommaso prove their artistic parkour skills in Istanbul and Cairo

overcome obstacles. That doesn't just sound cinematic, it actually is: ever since Foucan had a chase scene with James Bond in *Casino Royal* in 2006, the whole world has become familiar with the term freerunning.

All three sports may have their own unique histories, but they share some fundamental common ground: firstly, elegance of movement is— compared to other sports—far more important than the idea of competition. Secondly, their powerful momentum

had more to do with youth culture than athletic training. And lastly, they have permanently changed our perspective of the urban environment. Cities are now no longer a collection of houses, streets, stairs, and railings. They have been transformed into a limitless playground for children of all ages and for anyone who can see the true beauty and potential of obstacles: they can help you grow.

CURVED LINES

IMAGINATION AND FLOW IN BRAZIL'S SKATE SCENE

When Brazil's skateboarding pioneers took their first pushes in the late 1960s and early '70s, they did so in a hostile environment. From 1964 to 1985, Brazil was ruled by a military dictatorship under which youth culture, especially of the foreign-imported variety, was censured and sometimes repressed. So, with rebellion baked into its DNA, it's no surprise that skateboarding was seen as little more than vandalism by the authorities. While other Latin American countries, such as Mexico, were building state-funded skateparks, in the 1980s skateboarding was banned for a time in São Paulo.

With little infrastructure and the risk of being arrested if caught skating in the wrong place at the wrong time, Brazil's first skateboarders were imaginative and resilient. Recent governments have been more tolerant, but there are still few skateparks, so street skating rules supreme. Forced to work with what they have around them, Brazilian skaters regularly re-purpose existing architecture for their

own desires. In fact, many of São Paulo's architectural masterpieces have become popular spots and featured in skate edits, from the Oscar Niemeyer-conceived Ibirapuera Auditorium, which was an early mecca, to the *Espaço Cósmico* (Cosmic Space) sculpture in Praça da Sé.

São Paulo native Sandro Dias paid his respects to this tradition when he scaled the Ponte Estaiada—the elegant, two-level, 5,250-ft. (1,600-m) cable-stayed bridge designed by João Valente Filho—to ride a halfpipe 150 ft. (45 m) above moving traffic. Dias, also known as "King of the 540" and one of the few to have landed an upright 900, set up a 10-ft.-wide (3-m-wide) custom ramp between the bridge's vertical suspenders. He then climbed an unlit concrete stairway with just his board, a backpack, and a head torch, before popping out of a maintenance hatch to face a dizzying challenge. Overcoming understandable fear, Dias built up enough speed to pull off a backside air and write himself into Brazilian skateboarding history.

As six-time vert world champion, Dias is in a league of his own in Brazilian skateboarding. Similarly, no single person has made as profound an impact on Brazil's built environment as architect Oscar Niemeyer. While his contemporaries used concrete to construct straight-edged brutalist buildings, Niemeyer saw other possibilities, playing with concrete as if it was water. "I am not attracted to straight angles or to the straight line, hard and inflexible, created by man," Niemeyer once said. "I am attracted to free-flowing, sensual curves."

Niemeyer's vision might seem worlds away from that of a skateboarder's. But like a skateboarder humanizing the urban environment through movement and flow, Niemeyer looked at the city differently. The architect created from scratch: the curved lines of his elegant sketches were eventually cast into huge-scale reinforced concrete forms, while skateboarders take the chaos of the pre-existing environment and look to create fluid lines among the rough angles and inanimate forms.

CONCRETE DREAMS

SKATING THE UTOPIAN CREATIONS OF OSCAR NIEMEYER

Brazilian skateboarders Pedro Barros and Murilo Peres grew up looking at Niemeyer's UFO-like buildings and always dreamed of skating them. Miraculously, the pair were given rare permission for their *Concrete Dreams* project, which took them around the country, skating Niemeyer's iconic creations, from the National Congress in Brasília to the Contemporary Art Museum in Niterói.

Looking at Niemeyer's buildings through a skateboarder's eyes, there are glorious transitions everywhere. Unsurprisingly, given their revered status as emblems of architectural history and of Brazilian national identity, skating these buildings is strictly off-limits. But just like Niemeyer, Barros and Peres are dreamers determined to turn their ambitions into reality.

"There is a strong identity between the universe of this sport and Niemeyer's architecture and its values," explains Carlos Ricardo Niemeyer, executive superintendent of the Oscar Niemeyer Foundation, which granted Barros and Peres their wish. "Irreverence, freedom, the search for challenges, creativity in movement, all of this is in the essence of skateboarding as well as in Niemeyer's work, made of free, beautiful, and surprising curves."

ANARCHY IN THE COMUNA

THE CULTURAL REBIRTH OF A ONCE-NOTORIOUS NEIGHBORHOOD PROVES IDEAL TERRAIN FOR PASHA PETKUNS'S NO-RULES APPROACH TO PARKOUR

During the darkest days of Colombia's cocaine-fueled civil war in the 1980s and '90s, Comuna 13 was one of the world's most dangerous neighborhoods. Densely packed onto a hillside that rises to 5,000 ft. (1,500 m) above sea level, the maze-like settlement became a transit route in and out of Medellín for guerrillas, gangs, and paramilitaries. Today, Comuna 13, also known as San Javier, is a very different place and one of the most inspiring examples of urban regeneration anywhere in Latin America. Walls once riddled with bullets are now splashed with color: 800 murals by over 300 street artists have radically changed the face of the neighborhood. Crime has been displaced by culture, and Comuna 13 is now a mecca for musicians, break dancers, and even a 300-strong community of local freerunners.

"The architecture here is perfect for practicing parkour," says Latvian freerunner Pasha Petkuns, whose adventures in Colombia also include the capital, Bogotá. In Medellín, there has long been a stark difference between the gridded city in the valley below and the *comunas* (informal settlements), whose tightly packed red-brick houses with corrugated tin roofs cling to the hills. The transformation of poverty-stricken neighborhoods like Comuna 13 was brought about through radical experiments in urban planning and participatory forms of governance that began in earnest in the late 1990s.

Previously isolated from the rest of the city, Comuna 13 was reintegrated through the construction of elevated metros, cable cars, bridges, and escalators, which helped increase economic and social integration. Other architectural interventions included new libraries, schools, community buildings, and cultural centers. Together, these initiatives have helped to significantly reduce both violence and poverty. City authorities often choose to bulldoze "problematic" neighborhoods and start again. But in Medellín, the new architectural and social interventions co-exist with Comuna 13's original character. Like informal settlements elsewhere in Latin America and further afield, every piece of available space is used. Most houses were built by the residents themselves; electrical poles that resemble tangled spider webs are hooked up to power grids. With no central planning, the neighborhood grew organically into a dense constellation of rooftops, narrow passageways, and steep stairways—fruitful terrain for Petkuns.

The vibrancy of Comuna 13 owes much to its anarchic, "if it works, do it," evolution. Petkuns, too, has never been afraid to break the rules. "People told me I had to learn things a certain way," he reflects. "But if I want to slide on my face, I'll slide on my face. Who says I can't? Only you are limited by saying you have to land on your legs. The body is an instrument and you are playing it."

PARKOUR PIONEER

PASHA PETKUNS IS DETERMINED TO PUSH
AT THE LIMITS OF THE POSSIBLE

"I see opportunities everywhere," says Pasha Petkuns. "I love it so much, I don't need any drugs. Movement is the purest and cleanest drug for me." Raised in Daugavpils, Latvia, Petkuns knew he was born to move from an early age. "I grew up in a poor family, so I didn't have bicycles, skates, skateboards, or balls," he says. "That's why I use my body."

Petkuns was introduced to parkour in his teens through videos shown to him by a friend, and he went straight to work on a showreel. Released in 2009, the inventive and high-energy edit announced a major freerunning talent to the world. Fast-forward to today and Petkuns is at the very height of his game: he is a member of the elite Team Farang and the only person to have won three consecutive Red Bull Art of Motion Freerunning Championships. The irrepressible athlete is always thinking about ways to break boundaries and introduce parkour to new contexts, whether it's performing with Cirque du Soleil, or filming stunts for Hollywood. And in 2021, he broke ground leaping through the biggest freerunning set ever built: a 23-ton, 52-foot-high (16-meter-high) construction for his dazzling *Human Pinball* project.

QUEEN OF THE CASTILLO

MARIANA PAJÓN DEMONSTRATES WHY SHE REIGNS SUPREME ON THE BMX AT CARTAGENA'S CASTILLO DE SAN FELIPE DE BARAJAS

Sixty-eight cannons stare out over the Caribbean Sea from the Castillo de San Felipe de Barajas in Cartagena. The Spanish Empire began construction of this imposing fortress in 1536, solidifying control over what is now Colombia. Perched on the San Lázaro hill, the strategic location ensures the fortress dominates both land and sea approaches to Cartagena—should prospective invaders ever get close enough, they would have to overcome its considerable fortifications.

In the world of BMX, Colombian rider Mariana Pajón is equally dominant: few challengers ever get close. Nicknamed the "Queen of BMX," Pajón has two Olympic gold medals and six UCI World Championships, making her one of the most successful athletes in the history of the sport.

Raised in Medellín, Colombia, Pajón learned to ride when she was only three, rode her first race at the age of four, competed in her first international at five, and won her first world title when she was nine. She has often cited an inspirational quote by Eleanor Roosevelt as a guiding philosophy: "The future belongs to those who believe in the beauty of their dreams." Two years before the 2012 Olympic Games in London, Pajón tattooed the Olympic rings onto her wrist as a promise to herself that she would triumph. She won gold—and then successfully defended it in Rio in 2016.

ALL RIDE!

*THE IRREPRESSIBLE RISE OF SKATEBOARDING
AND BMX IN MEXICO CITY*

Skateboarding in Mexico got off to an earlier start than in most countries. The sport's spiritual home in Southern California neighbors Mexico, and with such strong cultural and commercial links between the two, the stoke inevitably slipped south across the border. The first Mexican skaters got rolling in the 1970s before there were any stores or skateparks. But the government quickly got behind them, building skateparks throughout the 1980s, partly as a way to breathe new life into degraded public spaces.

By understanding that skateboarding could play a role in urban regeneration, Mexico's government was ahead of its time—elsewhere in the world, many continue to ignore the benefits. There are regular conflicts between skateboarding communities and municipalities who don't see a place for the sport in their visions of an ideal city. All over the globe, skaters still have to fight for space. Yet while Mexico took an early lead in building skate infrastructure, half of the population was conspicuously left out: women and girls. Machismo is alive and well in Mexican society and for decades skateboarding—like much else—was an almost exclusively boy's club. It was frowned upon for women to skate or be involved with something perceived as a masculine activity. As skater and photographer Olga Aguilar told the *New York Times:* "We had to hide our skateboards because our mom didn't want us to skate."

Aguilar has been documenting the skateboarding scene in Mexico City since the 1980s. Throughout her time in the scene, she has worked to dismantle stigmas and bring more women into skateboarding. For a long time, Aguilar had few allies, but in recent years a seismic shift has occurred. Mexico City is now blowing up as a skateboarding destination and attracting increasing international attention. Global brands such as Vans and Nike Skateboarding have built skateparks, adding to the capital's extensive collection of parks for skaters of all levels—and BMX riders too. The heat also extends to the streets, with growing numbers of foreign and home-grown skate and BMX edits helping to draw attention to the city. A vibrant street life far less regimented than in the United States, coupled with a kaleidoscope of architectural styles, provides endless opportunity. Among the immense backdrops on offer are Aztec ruins, Spanish-colonial churches and palaces, and a dazzling array of 20th-century revolutionary, midcentury modern, and even Mayan Revival architecture.

But the most exciting aspect of Mexico City's skate scene today is its diversity. More women-led skateboarding schools are emerging, such as *Mujeres en Patineta* (Women on Skateboards), which teaches girls of all ages from low-income backgrounds how to skate. Its director, Mariana Muñoz, explains: "The social openness that exists here, as well as the women's movement, have allowed women's skate to grow in an unprecedented way."

CITY OF DREAMS

WITH PERFECT WEATHER, UNIQUE OUTDOOR SPACES, AND A DIVERSE CULTURE, LOS ANGELES MAKES EVERYTHING FEEL POSSIBLE

When Letícia Bufoni moved to Los Angeles at 14, it was a dream come true. "L.A. was always the dream city," she says. "It was in all the skate videos, and I always wanted to go and skate there." Bufoni is not alone in her love for the city. The year-round warm weather, unique outdoor spaces, and diverse culture make Los Angeles a magnet for skateboarders, BMX riders, and parkour athletes. "If we want to train outdoors every single day of the year, we can," says freerunner and L.A. native Sara Mudallal. "It's always beautiful outside."

Moving through the city, skateboarders see the world differently. Every building, every ramp, every staircase is an opportunity to launch a different trick. "Everything can be skateable," says Bufoni—she especially likes to skate on public school campuses. "There are schoolyards in L.A. that you can only find in L.A.," she says. After 1945, the population of Los Angeles grew quickly, and the city built schools with layouts that follow a cookie-cutter sameness. Covered hallways link single-story classroom buildings that open to outdoor courtyards and playing fields. There are picnic benches to tailslide, ramps to ollie, and staircases for high-flying kick flips. "They have everything," says Bufoni. When the final bell rings, the skateboarders move in.

And where there's skateboarding, there are invariably freerunners and BMX riders too. "People jumping from building to building is more of a European thing," says Mudallal. "In L.A., it's mainly the architectural structures that are built from the ground." Instead of looking up, parkour athletes find their spaces at ground level. At University of California, Los Angeles's Brentwood campus, square concrete blocks decorate a parking garage and form the perfect launchpad for jumps and flips.

In L.A. the car is king, and freeways form the circulatory system that connects the city's sprawling parts. An infrastructure of ramps and bridges creates an urban jungle where opportunities for play abound. Running through the heart of L.A., the 405 freeway connects the San Fernando Valley in the north to Orange County in the south. Near Culver City, a ramp off the 405 is one of L.A.'s best-known parkour spaces: the Pass-By fills the space between the Howard Hughes Parkway exit and the 405. "Everyone has been there," says Mudallal.

But it's not just the built environment that makes the city inviting—the people do, too. "Everything happens in Los Angeles, and you're skating with the best," says Bufoni, who owns a house in L.A. with a skatepark and miniramp in the backyard.

Mudallal was born in Santa Monica after her parents emigrated from Jordan. She wears a hijab and has found an acceptance in Los Angeles that she does not always feel in other cities. "Everyone understands this multicultural mosh pit that we're in," she says. "It's really cool living here." Mudallal hopes to become the first hijabi stunt woman to work in Hollywood. In Los Angeles, it feels like everything is possible.

Pink MOTEL
AIR CONDITIONED
BY REFRIGERATION
TV
CAFE
Red Bull
NIKE SB

FEARLESS AND FLY

STREET SKATEBOARDING WITH LETÍCIA BUFONI

Growing up in São Paulo, Letícia Bufoni learned to skateboard in the streets near her family home. She was nine years old when she got her first skateboard. After two months, Bufoni could ollie and land a pop shove-it. "I was the only girl skating with eight or ten boys," she says. Her father did not approve: one day, he sawed her skateboard in half. "My world was upside down."

But when a family friend convinced her to do a contest, Bufoni won. After that, her father changed his tune and traveled with a 14-year-old Bufoni to Los Angeles to compete in the X Games, where she finished eighth. Bufoni decided she wanted to stay in the United States and reluctantly, her family agreed. "At first it was really hard, because I didn't speak any English," she says. But Bufoni persevered, and she soon had a shoe sponsor. Since 2007, she has won six X Games gold medals and traveled the world to compete and film, building a reputation for a high-intensity style and fearless approach. In 2021, Bufoni represented Brazil in Tokyo at the Olympic Games and finished ninth. "When I started skating I just wanted to skate, because I was doing what I love," she says. "I never thought I'd be one of the biggest skaters in the world—it's just crazy."

WHERE GRAVITY RULES

WITH ITS STEEP TERRAIN AND TWISTING STREETS,
SAN FRANCISCO IS A HIGH-STAKES ROLLERCOASTER RIDE

From the top of Twin Peaks, San Francisco runs downhill in every direction. Perched precariously above the sea, streets tilt up at absurd angles, and the arduous terrain has made the city a proving ground for urban athletes.

"San Francisco is incredibly punishing whether you're on a track bike or a skateboard or a BMX bike," says Chas Christiansen, a bike messenger turned professional cyclist. Plunging downhill, streets snake through tight switchbacks for the ultimate thrill ride. "It's like they paved a rollercoaster," he says.

The city draws a talented and diverse crew. It's one thing to boardslide a rail on a skateboard; another to boardslide a rail, ollie a curb, and bomb down the steep roads of the Golden Gate City. A loose-knit crew of skateboarders known as GX1000 combine classic street skating tricks with daredevil speed runs. Sometimes a group of 50 or more skateboarders will swarm Market Street, one of the city's main drags, at 30 mph (50 km/h) per hour

or more—dodging cars, hopping trolley tracks, and hitting tricks all the way down.

Skateboarders share the city with fixed-gear bike riders—when San Francisco hosted the Cycle Messenger World Championship in 1996, messengers from New York City brought single-speed track bikes with them. Up to that point, San Francisco bike messengers typically rode mountain bikes for their durability, but the community quickly adapted to embrace the fast, simple track bikes. Designed to race on flat tracks, fixed-gear bikes do not have brakes; carving downhill like a snowboarder, riders skid first on one side, then the other in an effort to scrub speed. "Once you go over the edge of that hill, physics dictates what happens next; you're not stopping unless you jump off the bike," Christiansen says.

The thrill and risk factors attract a vibrant community that was documented in *MASH,* skate photographer Gabe Morford and filmmaker Mike Martin's 2007 film about the fixed-gear scene. Street skateboarders such as Julien

Stranger and John Cardiel got in on the local track-bike scene too. "There was this huge crossover, especially between the *Anti-Hero* and *Thrasher* magazine vibe and track bikes in San Francisco," Christiansen says. Graffiti artists such as ORFN worked as bike messengers and Barry McGee of the Mission School has designed skate decks and track bikes.

Visible from all over San Francisco, Twin Peaks rises 922 ft. (281 m) above sea level. Not far from the summit, a series of barriers traces the boundary between the road and the hill's steep drop. Tagged with graffiti, a mural memorializes GX1000 skateboarder Pablo Ramirez and marks the start of one of the best-known downhill street runs in San Francisco. Here, the characters who make up the city's street scene come together: graffiti artists, skateboarders, track-bike riders, and BMX riders. Whatever they ride, they all call San Francisco home and share a willingness to climb to the top of the highest hill, turn around, and place their fate in the hands of gravity.

FEEL THE BEAT

*TERRY ADAMS FUSES FLATLAND BMX ARTISTRY
WITH NEW ORLEANS JAZZ TRADITION*

In New Orleans, parades regularly wind through the streets of the French Quarter and Tremé. A parade may celebrate a wedding or a funeral, or it might simply be an excuse for music on a Sunday afternoon. Typically, a brass band playing jazz takes the lead; behind the band and other notables, a second line forms. A drummer riffs on the beats from the musicians up front as costumed dancers wave colorful handkerchiefs. The second line grows as the parade moves through the city's neighborhoods, and spectators are encouraged to join the party. Second-lining, an integral part of life in New Orleans, dates from the 19th century and remains an enduring tradition of Black American culture.

With its own form of free-flowing creativity, flatland BMX makes a good accomplice to the sound of New Orleans: jazz. In 2017, ahead of the Voodoo Jam event, Louisiana local Terry Adams brought together the artistry of flatland with the city's second-line tradition. Together with Viki Gómez, Matthias Dandois, Yohei Uchino, and Benjamin Hudson, Adams formed a second line, the crew synchronizing tricks with brass-band beats as they moved through the streets. "Each rider brought their own style," Adams says. "When you look at flatland, it's an art form that's infinite. It was about finding that rhythm—the right vibe—with everyone."

Growing up, Adams rode BMX bikes with the kids in his Hammond, Louisiana, neighborhood. By the age of 11, he was riding ramps and learning freestyle moves. "The first time I saw flatland, it felt like I was dreaming, because all the tricks they were doing just looked impossible," he says. Flatland does not require much space—any flat area of pavement will work. Spending long nights in his mom's driveway or out in the street in front of his grandmother's house, Adams turned his dream into a reality. "I wanted to know what it felt like to be able to float around the bike like that," he says. "I became obsessed with learning it." He began competing in flatland contests at the age of 16.

Adams has since won an X Games gold medal and the NORA Cup twice. When his son Ledge was born in 2018, he felt he had reached a crossroads in his career. "I started looking at all the trophies on the wall, and I thought I could either keep pushing forward or slow down," he says. "I'm really glad I decided to push forward." During his long career, he has traveled all over the world for contests and exhibitions: "It has definitely opened my eyes to see where I can actually bring flatland BMX." Adams has ridden in the shadow of the Eiffel Tower in Paris and in the dried-out bed of the Los Angeles River. But with the second-line project, he returned home to Louisiana. "Bringing flatland BMX together with the traditional brass-band parades of New Orleans for a riding project was so wild and unique," he says. "Putting the two things together was very powerful."

RIDE THE RHYTHM

NEW YORK CITY INSPIRES FREERUNNERS AND BIKE LIFE RIDERS TO CREATE ART IN MOTION

New York City moves to its own beat. Traffic bustles and flows. Sidewalks teem with people heading to work, school, or play. Above, buildings stack up like peaks in a mountain range, each higher than the next, while roads cut through the deep canyons they create. It's easy to feel insignificant in a landscape like this, but across the five boroughs, New York's urban athletes fearlessly make their mark on the city.

Ostensibly, New York City is an improbable place to ride a bike. Yet Bike Life—a loose community of riders— thrives. Ride-outs draw anywhere from 10 to 100 riders, often even more. Word passes through social media and neighborhood grapevines. The bike brings all kinds of people who find common ground in the joy of riding together. "Bikes unify everyone," says Jae Milez. "I've seen gang members come together all for the love of riding." Young Latino and Black men form most of the Bike Life community, but ride-outs welcome everyone. "This is not just a guy's sport," says Curly, a female rider from the Lower East Side.

Bike Life prizes style and creativity. Holding their front wheels high in the air, some riders can wheelie an entire city block or more. Milez has become so proficient at riding a wheelie, he will sometimes not bother with a front wheel at all. Other riders dodge and weave through traffic, swerving at the last possible moment to avoid collisions with cars and pedestrians. The skills required to ride in New York City, never mind the wheelies and tricks, take practice to master. Curly started riding in 2017. "At first, I was embarrassed," she says. "I practiced alone in the parking lot before deciding to step out of my comfort zone."

While the Bike Life riders move through the city streets, freerunners test their bodies in unexpected spaces: curved railings in Battery Park City invite jumps and flips. At the Heckscher Playground in Central Park, natural rock features connect seamlessly with play structures. The possibilities for flow lines are infinite. In Times Square, neon signs wink, cars honk, and tourists snap photos. Amid the chaos, a parkour athlete finds focus and adapts his body to the unique shapes and forms of the city. A train passes over Williamsburg Bridge. High above hangs a freerunner, dwarfed by the bridge's massive structures. Using their bodies, they create art on a human scale.

With their Bike Life crew, riders such as Curly and Milez roll to the city's rhythms. For them, the bike offers a vehicle for self-expression and freedom: "It was like destiny," Curly says. "You know when something is just meant for you." Freerunners find that same self-expression in shaping their bodies to fit the city's landscape. Out on the bike or climbing high, they make New York City their own.

SKATEBOARDING IS LIFE

TJ ROGERS SHOWCASES THE VARIETY OF SKATEBOARDING IN CANADA

In downtown Vancouver, four bronze figures stand in front of the BC Place stadium. The sculptures memorialize Terry Fox, who set out to run across Canada after losing his right leg to cancer. Fox spent five months running the Marathon of Hope, raising $24.2 million for cancer research before his death in Thunder Bay, Ontario. His determination turned him into a national hero. A flat plaza surrounds the statues, and for skateboarders like TJ Rogers, it's an irresistible invitation.

From his troubled childhood to his success as a professional skateboarder, Rogers understands the power of determination. "That's what skateboarding is about: it's striving to do better for yourself," he says. Growing up in Whitby, Ontario, with parents who struggled with addiction, Rogers threw his energy into skateboarding, waking up early to skate before school. "If I didn't have skating, I don't know what I would have done." After moving to Los Angeles, Rogers turned professional. "Every time I step on that skateboard, it's like the first day again," he says. "Skateboarding is my life."

Such commitment is familiar to Aaron Cayer, co-owner of Birling Skate Shop in Ottawa. Cayer is among the advocates in Canada who want to make skateboarding more accessible. Through his organization, For Pivot's Sake, he collects used skateboards and donates them. "We give them to people who may not have the money to buy them, along with free classes," says Mégane Legault-Leclair, who works at Birling. "We're trying to create a safe space for anyone who wants to access skateboarding."

A similar goal motivates Marie Anne Louis-Charles, who created "Girls, Gays, and Theys" skate sessions in Montréal and whose gatherings feature skills practice and art swaps. "I just want everyone to get into skateboarding," says Louis-Charles. "I want to skate with other girls, and I want to skate with queer people, and I want to be in a space with other people like myself."

Across the country in Vancouver, photographer Norma Ibarra turns her lens toward women and marginalized communities in skateboarding. "I want to look at a magazine and see more women, more people of color, and more trans skaters," she says. She can often be found at likely the most famous skatepark in Canada, the Vancouver Skate Plaza, which lies under two freeway overpasses. Graffiti covers the bridges' stanchions, which blend into the park's features. Nine hours east, in Kootenay, Daniel "Alien" Nelson built Driftopia, one of Canada's many DIY skateparks. Surrounded by towering pines, the heart-shaped bowl commemorates the life of Nelson's longtime friend Josh Evin. "It's a sanctuary," Nelson says. The contrast between the urban Skate Plaza and Nelson's passion project shows the rich variety of the Canadian scene.

Whether he's pushing along a boardwalk with the Toronto skyline behind him, hitting an ollie over the head of a sculpture in Calgary, or boardsliding in the shadow of the Canadian Rockies in Banff, Rogers has traveled a long way from the skatepark in Whitby.

But his hometown still holds a piece of his heart. "Every time I'm back here, it's like I'm back in my serenity," Rogers says.

ATHLETES

PHOTO CREDITS

BIOGRAPHIES

Charlie Allenby is a London-based journalist. He spent his formative years obsessed with 20" wheeled bikes—whether it was playing *Dave Mirra Freestyle BMX* on the PlayStation, reading *Ride BMX* magazine, or sessioning his local trails—before adding road, gravel, and mountain biking to his now lifelong passion. He has written about cycling for publications including the *Guardian,* the *Independent,* and *Rouleur* and is the author of *Bike London: A Guide to Cycling in the City* (ACC Art Books, 2021).
Playtime; Barcelona, Birmingham, Dubai, Edinburgh, Lisbon, London, Pamplona, Paris, Prague
pp. 4–7, 11, 38, 45, 54, 61, 65, 71, 73, 74, 88, 93, 116, 120

A resident of Salzburg, Austria, **Günter Baumgartner** is a (sports) journalist and content agency owner. He has a soft spot for all types of ball games, U.S. sports, and urban sports, including freerunning and breaking. In his leisure time, he can be found on the mountain and on his mountain bike almost as often as on tennis and squash courts and the soccer field. He also enjoys playing both indoor hockey and ice hockey and spending time on the ski slopes.
Amsterdam, Frankfurt, Tokyo / Osaka
pp. 28, 31, 32, 37, 130

Iain Borden is Professor of Architecture and Urban Culture at the Bartlett School of Architecture, University College London. He is the author of *Skateboarding and the City: A Complete History* (Bloomsbury, 2019). His research explores the experience of architecture and cities, and particularly of urban space through movement, film, and photography.
New Forms of Liberation
pp. 94–100

Konstantin Butz is a researcher and lecturer at the Academy of Media Arts Cologne, Germany. He has studied American studies and cultural studies at the University of Bremen and at Dickinson College in Carlisle, Pennsylvania. He holds a doctorate degree in American studies from the University of Cologne. His publications include *Skateboard Studies* (Koenig Books, 2018) and *Grinding California: Culture and Corporeality in American Skate Punk* (transcript, 2012).
Always Already a Playground
pp. 46–52

Writer and author **Howard Calvert** spends his spare time ultra running, mountain biking, and walking his Nova Scotia duck-tolling retriever through the wilds of southern England. He has run ultramarathons and sky races in the Scottish Highlands, the Pennines, the South Downs, Mont Blanc, the Dolomites, the Austrian Alps, and British Columbia, and hopes to keep going until his hips and/or knees give way.
Venice
p. 15

Titus Dittmann is a skateboard pioneer and entrepreneur, racer, former teacher, keynote speaker, youth lobbyist, skydiver, university lecturer, media darling, and above all an influencer with skate-aid, an organization promoting the educational power of skateboarding in the context of worldwide youth-aid projects.
Kampala
pp. 150, 157

Alex King is a British journalist and documentary producer based in Athens and London. He covers humanitarian issues, activism, and alternative culture. He is the author of *Soul of Athens: A Guide to 30 Exceptional Experiences* (Jonglez, 2021) and is currently editing *Tight,* a feature documentary on Indian bodybuilding.
Taking the Reins; Cairo, Cape Town, Cartagena, Istanbul, Johannesburg, Lagos, Medellín / Bogotá, Mexico City, Moscow, São Paulo / Brasília / Niterói
pp. 83, 87, 103, 109, 111, 122–128, 136, 142, 159, 161, 162, 167, 176, 181, 186, 191, 193, 197

Originally from the U.K., **Dave Morgan** now resides in Berlin. A skateboarder and creative, he has worked for publications including *Free Skate Magazine* and *Vague Magazine.* He has spent years traveling Europe through skateboarding and works in the skateboarding industry alongside his journalistic work.
Berlin
p. 21

Raised in Bonn, Germany, **Jens Schnabel** is a former skateboard / snowboard pro, the editor-in-chief of *Monster Skateboard Magazine,* a team manager, international sales manager, host/moderator, journalist, and author. France, Italy, California. Back to Germany. And today, skate-aid.
Kampala
pp. 150, 157

Jen See is a writer based in Santa Barbara, California. She has contributed to numerous publications including *The Red Bulletin, Men's Journal,* and *Outside Magazine.* Her interests span from skateboarding to fitness to travel. She has a PhD in U.S. history, and, when not at work, she can most likely be found outside, surfing or mountain biking.
Los Angeles, New Orleans, New York City, San Francisco, Vancouver / Toronto
pp. 202, 207, 212, 217, 221, 228

Andreas Wollinger has been a journalist for weekly and monthly magazines for over 40 years. A native of Vienna, he started out at *Wochenpresse* and was later editor-in-chief at *WIENER* and *Wienerin, Woman, E-Media, Seitenblicke Magazin,* and *Terra Mater.* He currently works as a writer and chief editor at Red Bull Media House, with a focus on *The Red Bulletin* and *Pragmaticus.*
Smells Like Teen Spirit; Berlin
pp. 22, 168–174

URBAN PLAYGROUNDS

*ATHLETES CLAIM CITIES
AROUND THE WORLD*

Conceived and edited by
gestalten and **Benevento Publishing**

Design and layout by **gestalten**

Edited by **Robert Klanten**
and **Laura Alllsop**

Editorial Management by
Arndt Jasper and **Stefan Mayr**

Texts by **Charlie Allenby,
Günter Baumgartner, Iain Borden,
Konstantin Butz, Howard Calvert,
Titus Dittmann, Alex King,
Dave Morgan, Jens Schnabel,
Jen See,** and **Andreas Wollinger**

English translations by **WeSwitch GmbH,
Romina Russo Lais, Heather B. Bock**

Design by **Isabelle Emmerich**
Layout and cover by **Charlotte Bourdeix**
and **Melanie Ullrich**
Production by **Benedikt Lechner**

Photo Editor: **Madeline Dudley-Yates**

Typefaces: *Timmons NY 2.0* by
Matt Willey and *Franklin Gothic ATF*
by **Morris Benton**

Cover image by **Vincent Perraud /
Red Bull Content Pool**
Backcover images by **Ben Franke** (top),
**Mauricio Ramos /
Red Bull Content Pool** (center),
**Atiba Jefferson /
Red Bull Content Pool** (right), and
Yuyu Matsui (bottom)

Printed by **Finidr,** Czech Republic
Made in Europe

Published by gestalten, Berlin 2022
ISBN 978-3-96704-041-8

For more information, and to order
books, please visit www.gestalten.com

Bibliographic information published
by the Deutsche Nationalbibliothek.
The Deutsche Nationalbibliothek
lists this publication in the
Deutsche Nationalbibliografie;
detailed bibliographic data is
available online at www.dnb.de

None of the content in this book was
published in exchange for payment
by commercial parties or designers;
the inclusion of all work is based solely
on its artistic merit.

This book was printed on paper
certified according to the standards
of the FSC®.

MIX
From responsible
sources
FSC® C014138